# Memories of a
# LIFE IN THE ARMY

# Memories of a
# LIFE IN THE ARMY

Major General Louis W. Prentiss, Jr.

# MEMORIES OF A LIFE IN THE ARMY

*iUniverse books may be ordered through booksellers or by contacting:*

*iUniverse*
*1663 Liberty Drive*
*Bloomington, IN 47403*
*www.iuniverse.com*
*1-800-Authors (1-800-288-4677)*

*ISBN: 978-1-4917-5721-5 (sc)*
*ISBN: 978-1-4917-5720-8 (e)*

*Library of Congress Control Number: 2015900777*

*Printed in the United States of America.*

*iUniverse rev. date:   02/05/2015*

# Contents

# Preface

How did all of these memory vignettes get started? One Christmas I received a beautiful leather-bound book from Barbara. This book is intended for one in their waning years to put all sorts of family information in it so that it won't be lost to future generations. It included a three-generation family tree and questions such as "Who influenced you the most?" I have never had the talent for penmanship, and as I get older it gets poorer (unlike my father who had strong, beautiful handwriting). I at first thought of filling in each page using the computer and printer but discarded that idea for two reasons; it wouldn't look too good, and I didn't like the forced structure of the book. Rather than hand-write three generations of the family tree, I refer those who are interested to the Prentiss family tree that is posted on the Internet. Go to http://tribalpages.com and enter *Prentiss* as the user id. This work goes back twenty-one generations to someone called Berengarius, who begot Papa de Valios, who begot William I Longsword, Duke of Normandy and so on.

One Christmas evening I was born an Army Brat. I spent eighteen years as a Brat until I entered West Point and became an Army West Point Cadet. After four years I became a commissioned officer in the US Army. Thirty-one years later I retired from the Army and became a member of the US Army, Retired. Thus, from the moment I was born until the day I die I will have been a member of the army. These vignettes cover those special memories that keep coming back to me.

The first vignette that I did was titled "My Brother." I wrote this initially only for myself. I had wanted to do something like this for over fifty years but could never get my feelings together to be able to put them on paper. One morning in Steamboat Springs, Colorado, I sat down at the computer and completed it in less than an hour. There was no editing of it; the way it reads now is original. After a few days I decided to send it to the extended family. I received responses from some of the family that they wanted me to write more. I chose to write "Reno" because it had such a strange twist to it. "Omaha" was a natural next because it tied into "Reno" so there was some continuity. It seemed that writing them in reverse order was easier because I already knew what was next. Those in the family who responded to the vignettes have encouraged me to continue and have offered suggestions as to what they want included.

I did a six-hour videotape of my mother about thirteen years before her death. It covers in my mother's words her life from *A* to *Z*. When I did "My Father and Mother" I did not repeat what is in the tapes but gave my reactions. If only I could have recorded six hours on my father.

If I were to say where my home was when I was growing up, I would have to say Fort Belvoir, Virginia. It never felt that way, but that is where I lived the most until I retired. It wasn't called Belvoir when I first lived there; instead, it was Fort Humphreys, named after a former Chief of Engineers. (It was renamed Fort Belvoir in the mid-thirties.) Pop had just transferred to the Corps of Engineers and we moved twenty-five miles south of Fort Myer, VA. Pop told me that he held several positions there, including the Provost Marshal, Supply Officer, and the Signal Officer—all at the same time. He played polo, and Mother was also an equestrian. In Mother's attic when she died was a footlocker with blue and red ribbons she had won in competition. She was an excellent jumper, for there was a rather large silver cup in the locker that had her name engraved upon it.

I remember very little of Fort Humphreys, but my earliest memories of life are here. We lived in a wood frame house that had been built during WWI. What I do remember is that it had a screened porch. A single seat swing hung from the ceiling by two chains. My mother had an Uncle Ernest, a widower, who was nearly deaf. He wore earpieces that were connected by wire to a battery-operated amplifier he kept in his left breast pocket. Uncle Ernest came to Sunday dinner one time, and he, Catharine, and I were on the porch. I got in the swing, got it going well, and kept calling to Uncle Ernest to watch me. He was busy with Catharine and ignored me regardless of how loud I yelled. My swinging exploits were never appreciated by Uncle Ernest. Later Mother told me that he was very selective as to what he wanted to hear. Again, these are my earliest memories of life.

When chapters were finished, I e-mailed them to family members and to friends and classmates who had expressed an interest in reading them. I have included comments that clarify or add to my memories. I am indebted for their feedback. Earl Dille, a '50 grad from Annapolis, has been a friend for twenty-five years. Lt. Col. Larry Applebaum lives in Germany and has been an e-mail pen pal for fifteen years. Carl Baswell was not only a contemporary but also my partner in business. Dean Paquette and I served together in Korea, Vietnam, the Pentagon, the Engineer Advance Course, and The National War College. Dave Pettit, Tom Loper, and Ed West were both West Point classmates and Engineer Officers. Walt Plummer, Catharine's husband, is a 1948 West Point grad. Walt did a fabulous job finding errors and adding his experiences where ours touched. Helen Lee is Catharine and Walt's oldest daughter. She is married to Fred Lee, a retired Armor Officer and Army Brat. Chris Brittingham is Barbara's younger son who is serving in the Coast Guard. Penni Long, from Anthem, Arizona, used her talents to guide me and to edit my drafts. Jim Martin, Shirley's son, has helped in pulling all of the pieces together and printing them. Lastly, Shirley needs to be recognized in putting up with me as I buried myself in the den huddled over the computer.

As *Memories* evolves, each vignette remains open for additions and corrections. Since this is a work of my memories, there has been no research done and therefore there may be factual errors. If one discovers such errors, I would be happy to make corrections.
Lou Prentiss
lprentiss2@cox.net

December 2014

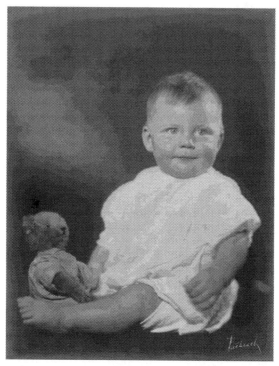

Me at eight months – 1928. I still have the teddy bear.

Eddie, Mother, Happy, Catharine – 1930

Pop's first photo as a 2nd Lt. – 1921

# Illustrations

# Chapter 1 – First Move: Golden, Colorado

My father entered Colorado School of Mines after graduating from Western High School, Washington D.C. Pop was first, or close to first, in his class in high school, Colorado School of Mines and the Command and General Staff College at Fort Leavenworth. He was commissioned in 1921 and returned in 1931 as the assistant professor of Military Science and Tactics (PMS&T). We arrived in Golden from Fort Humphreys. I was only four years old at the time and hadn't started school. When I turned five I entered kindergarten and can remember my first day of school. I am sure that very few people can remember their first day of school, but I can. The teacher had us stand up and tell the class what our names were and what our fathers did. When my time came I stood and said "My name is Happy and my father is in the army." My teacher knew who I was and that Pop was the assistant PMS&T at Mines and she said, "Your father is wicked because he is in the army and owns a gun." I never realized my father was wicked until then. This period was the start of the Great Depression and there were several political movements going on in the country. The Communist party was getting into full swing and there was a strong pacifist's movement as well. It seems that not too much has changed with Colorado educators from what I read about some of UC's professors. I recovered from my day one at school and rediscovered that my father wasn't wicked after all.

Mineralogy was taught in the basement of Guggenheim Hall. I attended these classes from the outside in that there were windows at ground level that were always open. I would pull the little red wagon—perhaps the same one I was hauled around in when we played "funeral"—up to one of the windows and sat listening to the mineralogy classes. The professor had a grand collection of rock specimens that he would pass around the class as he spoke of each one and how it was formed. When the specimens came around to the student near my window he would pass them up to me for my inspection. If they looked good, I would toss them in the wagon and haul them home. I got pretty good at identifying various rocks. When we were packing up to move to Fort Scott the mineralogy professor asked my father if he could have his specimen collection back. He came over and got them but left me with two samples of agate, beautifully polished, that I still have. When we were in Reno I sold subscriptions of the *Nevada Mining News*. As a reward, I won a boxed collection of all Nevada minerals. It was one of my prized collections, but I guess it was thrown away with my feathered headdress and bow and arrow (see San Francisco).

The Colorado School of Mines was sort of a rough and tumble school. At the start of school an initiation exercise was conducted on the freshmen class. At West Point we called it *hazing*. The freshmen were required to climb the mountain to the west of town and whitewash the big *M* made up of large boulders. After that the fraternities set up gauntlet runs manned by upperclassmen with paddles. I asked Pop if he ever had to run through one of these, and he smiled and said *yes*, that he had sat in a tub of salt water several days prior to the event. He was an SAE. After the running of the gauntlets, the freshmen went on a rampage—pelting upperclassmen with tomatoes, eggs, or anything else that would make a mess. I thought that going to college would be fun. Last year I drove into Golden and the big *M* was still there and as white as ever. I wonder if the fraternities still have paddles.

One day Eddie and Catharine decided that it would be a good idea to haul each other up the side of the two-storied house (I was later told by Catharine that this was a barn in back of the house) with a long rope that Eddie had obtained somewhere. He dangled the rope out of the window and Catharine would hold on to it and be pulled up to the window and then climb in. She would do the same for him. I complained that it was my turn and so both of them got on the top end and I hung onto the bottom. All went well until I got to the top and wasn't able to climb in the window. I finally let go and plummeted to the ground below. Our maid, Arlie, a full-blooded Cherokee Indian from Oklahoma, was doing the dishes in the kitchen below. She looked up to see me come flying past the window vertically. Out she came whooping and yelling at Eddie and Catharine as to what they had done to their little brother. My parents were away and Arlie was in charge of us. It all turned out well. I wasn't hurt or even scratched. I guess I just went limp.

Golden was a good place for kids to grow up. There was lots of open space with trees for climbing and relatively few cars. It was a pretty safe environment to let the kids run. I would go walking with my father on the outskirts of town, which was high plains grassland. There were rather wide irrigation ditches running to the farms that were scary for me. The water flowed quickly, the banks were high, and the ditches were wide. All of this was from the perspective of a five-year-old. Pop would grab me by the hand and leap across what was certain death to me. It was scary enough for me to remember it some seventy-five years later.

With the open spaces Eddie, Catharine, and the rest of the kids on the block played lots of outdoor games. My favorite was always *kick the can*. Hide and seek was not much fun but follow the leader was. Eddie usually was selected as the leader and I was always the last of the followers. One day, Eddie led us across a vacant lot that had an incinerator in the middle. This was made of concrete block with ramps leading up and down and a manhole cover at the top. Folks in the neighborhood would use the incinerator to burn paper and whatever. Eddie led us up the incinerator ramp, jumped over the manhole cover and down the other side. When I got to the top I stepped on the cover and it flipped—sending me inside. The cover then returned to its original position. Someone had burned something that morning, so there were still live ashes in the bottom. None of the kids had seen what had just happened to me. I was just missing. All of a sudden the lid opened up and arms reached down and pulled me out. A neighbor had been at her sink and had seen what happened to me and rushed out to get me. I got a few burns, but my favorite baseball cap got destroyed. I wrote a theme paper in junior high school about this experience and titled it *In the Fiery Furnace*. I think I got a C.

Pop always had a car. I think the one in Golden was a 1931 Ford. But it was one of them before the Ford that was of most interest. Although I don't remember it, my mother described it for me one time. It was a 1924

3

Cord that had been owned by Admiral Byrd, the Arctic explorer. How Pop got it and whether he was the second owner, I don't know. Mother described it as having the steering wheel covered with white cord tied with complicated nautical knots. Last year in Phoenix we attended an antique auction where some later model Cords were auctioned off. This particular car with its unique history would have easily brought in more than a quarter of a million dollars. Pop was smart but lacked the foresight to realize the treasure he had in the garage.

Golden with red wagon – 1932

# Chapter 2 – To the Pacific: San Francisco, California

Pop was selected to be aide-de-camp to brigadier general (BG) Cheney, who was the commanding general of Fort Scott, the Presidio of San Francisco. This was a coast artillery post and General Cheney was an engineer and a former commandant of the Engineer School. I thought this was strange and asked my father why an engineer was commanding a coast artillery post. He said that general officers were generalists and as such could be assigned to any general officer position in the army. If you compare today's assignments to those in 1932, you would not expect a thirty-three-year-old officer to be the aide-de-camp to a BG. A thirty-three-year-old today is probably already a major, and if he were to be an aide, it would be to a three-star lieutenant general. Such is the way of inflation.

We lived in a nice house on post, 33B, which had separate garages. As cars were driven out of their garages in the morning, padlocks were left hanging unlocked on the hasp so that they could be conveniently locked in the evening. All locks were identical since they were Government Issue. One morning I went along the row of garages, collected all of the padlocks, and brought them home. My mother saw them and ordered me to march right back out and put them where they belonged, to which I obediently complied. The only problem was that I didn't know which was which. The next morning there was great consternation from those trying to go to work. The previous evening they had driven in their garages and snapped the locks shut. No key worked the next morning. The only solution was that they all stood by the garages and traded out keys until they would find one that worked. My father heard about that for some time.

But that wasn't the biggest thing that happened to the garages. Eddie started a club, co-ed, which required the breaking of three garage windows in order to be inducted. The person who had the most broken windows was the president, with the vice president having the next highest to his or her credit. Eddie was way out in front with Catharine the runner up. I only qualified as a member with three kills because we ran out of windows. So the Prentiss family had three members in this club, including the president and vice president. It took about a day for the Military Police to track down the whole gang, and all of us were marched down to the MP station for questioning. Eddie and Catharine were quickly singled out as the ringleaders. All of the fathers were notified of the infractions and told to pick up their children at the MP station. The end result was that the fathers had to pay for the reglazing of the garages.

I was in the first grade then and really enjoyed school. Once a day the teacher would form a band with each of us getting various instruments—a triangle with a striking bar, a drum, two blocks with sandpaper glued to one side, a pair of cymbals, and various instruments that you would hum into rather than blow into. I always preferred the sand blocks. This was the start of my musical appreciation training. It didn't start up again until the seventh grade in Reno when I tried to join the band with Eddie's Boy Scout bugle. The teacher was very understanding and let me use a baritone and a trombone. Also, my only starring role in the theater was with the same teacher. She decided to put on a play using Henry Wadsworth Longfellow's "Song of Hiawatha" as the theme. I was selected to be Hiawatha, and the prettiest girl in the class was Minnehaha. I guess Minnehaha was my first girlfriend if you know the story. The play started with:

"By the shores of Gitche Gumee,
By the shining Big-Sea-Water, Stood the wigwam of Nokomis, Daughter of the Moon, Nokomis.
Dark behind it rose the forest,
Rose the black and gloomy pine-trees,
Rose the firs with cones upon them;
Bright before it beat the water,

Beat the clear and sunny water,
Beat the shining Big-Sea-Water."

Then, somewhere along the line I had my big part:
"Wah-wah-taysee, little fire-fly, little, flitting, white-fire insect,
Little, dancing, white-fire creature,
Light me with your little candle,
Ere upon my bed I lay me,
Ere in sleep I close my eyelids!"

From that point on, my father would say "By the shores of Gitche Gumee" any time we drove by a lake and "Wah-wah-taysee" in the evenings when the fireflies came out. I had my headdress of feathers and a bow and arrow (with suction cup points) for many years until they were tossed out in a move.

Golden Gate Bridge was under construction but not completed until a couple of years after we moved to Omaha. It was really interesting to see it go up. I have been fascinated by bridges ever since. My grandfather was given a small section of one of the cables as a paperweight. I have it on my desk. Fort Scott is right at the southern tip of the Golden Gate and was there to protect the harbor. There were sixteen-inch coastal battery emplacements around the fort. I don't think any were ever fired in anger, and I'm not sure if they were ever fired at all. To my knowledge they were never fired when we were there. They were fun to play around. A kid my size could crawl completely inside one of those 16- inchers.

Eddie had a magazine route selling *The Saturday Evening Post*. Every Saturday he would get a stack of magazines delivered to him and he would put them in a canvas-carrying bag and start out walking his route making deliveries. I used to love to walk with him, and he would always fuss that I couldn't keep up. One morning he kept calling me a *little fart*. I didn't know any bad words at the time and wouldn't until the fourth grade. That evening at the dinner table I blurted out that Eddie was calling me a little fart. My father blew water across the table, Catharine looked big-eyed, Eddie sort of slouched down in his chair, and my mother sat up very straight and told Eddie not to refer to me in such a manner. This was one of those grand moments when you accomplish the ultimate *gotcha*, and

I did it by ignorance. Mother was a Victorian's Victorian. She was very proper and never used coarse language. In fact, she never referred to a chicken or turkey thigh. It was always *the second joint*. Somehow *thigh* was a bit risqué for her to say. I think her father was responsible for setting her standards. She told me that once when she was a very little girl, she and a neighbor boy were wrestling in the front yard; her father came outside, whacked the boy with his cane, and then gave my mother one to boot. Can't do that nowadays.

Mother's parents lived across the bay in Berkeley. To get there we had to take the ferry from San Francisco and then the Shaddock Avenue electric train, getting off at Contra Costa Avenue. Grandfather was a meteorologist who worked for the Weather Bureau. He was quite renowned in his field and was the regional chief of the bureau in San Francisco. One can read his extensive biography on the Internet by putting in Edward Hall Bowie in Google and selecting his name from the NOAH site. He was commissioned a major in WWI and served as the meteorologist for the American Expedition Force in Europe. He kept his title after the war and was always referred to as Major Bowie. I have his major leafs and crossed flags (Signal Corps) that he wore with my insignia collection. When I would visit my grandparents I would always walk to the train stop in the evening to meet Grandfather. He really liked that and would "salt" the sidewalk with quarters that he would flip when I wasn't looking. By the time we got to the house I would have found fifty to seventy-five cents. The next day I would go out looking and never could find more. One time I saw what he was doing, but I never let on that I knew. Thus the quarters kept coming.

I was born on Christmas day. My folks had gone to Pop's mother's home for Christmas dinner and in the afternoon Mother started to feel signs of the coming event. So, out to Walter Reed Hospital they went. I was born at 11:40 p.m. I always felt that I was someone special being born on Christmas, sort of like being a direct descendant of Jesus. All of my life I have gotten comments like "Your mother really had a Christmas present, didn't she? Ha-ha-ha!" and "You really got gypped on presents, didn't you? Ha-ha-ha!" Everyone thought that he was original, but I have heard the same comments a billion times.

I have always said that if you are to be born in December, it is best to be born on Christmas because everyone remembers the date and makes sure that you don't get gypped. I never got a present that said *for your birthday and Christmas.* However, there was one aspect of being born on Christmas that bothered me and that was that I never had a birthday party with my friends. I brought this up to my parents and told them that I wanted to switch my birthday to the fourth of July so I could have a party. The summer of 1934 my birthday was officially switched. All of the gift-giving relatives were duly notified, the packages came rolling in, and I had a great party ending with fireworks. I was pleased with my choice of birthdays. But in November when all of the department stores started their Christmas displays with Christmas music, I felt some misgivings that I had lost something special. I told my parents that I wanted to reclaim my original birthday and keep it forever and ever. The word went out to the gift-giving relatives of the change. I had a double birthday with double presents that year. Years later I read a story about the author Robert Louis Stevenson. A little girl was bemoaning the fact that she had been born on Christmas and so Stevenson switched birthdays with her. He got the better deal.

The really good gift-giving relatives consisted on my mother's side of her parents and two sisters with families and on my father's side, his mother, his sister and brother—both with families. Mother's sister was married to a lawyer named Ralph Wallace who lived in San Diego, California and had three boys: Bill, Ralph (called Sandy because of his hair) and Ed (called Bunny). How would you like to be a boy and have your friends know you were called Bunny? In my family we never combined gifts with a present going out *from all of us.* Gift giving was a very personal thing. We all got allowances and we were expected to either make or buy presents using our own money. We were also expected to wrap and tag each. My parents were responsible for bundling them up, placing them in a box, addressing the box, and sending it off. The weeks just prior to Christmas the boxes would start coming in. I kept track of each as to size and origin. One year on Christmas Eve I announced that we had not received a box from the Eggos. There was a look of puzzlement on all faces. My mother asked, "Who are the Eggos?" I said, "You know, the Eggos, my cousin Sandy Eggo."

Eddie, commanding the gang with fixed bayonets. I am
on the left. Garages are in the background.
Fort Scott – 1934

Eddie, again in command. Fort Scott – 1934

## Comments

# Chapter 3 – Midwest: Omaha, Nebraska

Omaha in the mid thirties was, to me, the hottest and the coldest place on earth. We came to Omaha from San Francisco where the weather was either cool and sunny or cool and foggy.

There was nothing like the oppressive heat and humidity or cold and wind that greeted me in Omaha. My father had been transferred from Fort Scott, the Presidio of San Francisco to the Omaha district of the Corps of Engineers. This type army life was all new to me in that there were no soldiers, army trucks, or parades. There was Fort Omaha, where you could find a soldier, as well as a PX and commissary. I think that Fort Omaha was left over from the Indian wars. The Omaha district was responsible for the navigation and flood control projects on most of the upper Missouri River. Pop worked in civilian clothes rather than in uniform. There were two or three other officers in the district; Tom and Bernie Loper's father, Doc Loper, was the district engineer. One of the good things was that family members were authorized to go on these inspection trips. My favorite venture was to travel the Missouri River on one of the two riverboats that the district owned, the *Sgt. Floyd*, a steam powered stern paddle wheeler and the *Sgt. Pryor*, steam powered but screw driven. Sergeants Pryor and Floyd were members of the Lewis and Clark expedition and so it was fitting to name these boats for them.

These boats were steel hull flat-bottomed boats designed specifically for use in the Missouri River where sand bars were constantly shifting. Their draft was only about four feet and they could easily slide on and off a sand bar without any damage. When that happened, the skipper would throw the paddle wheels in reverse with lots of power and pull her off. When the skipper noticed an unusual flow pattern, he would station a crewmember in the bow with a lead line to take soundings. You would hear "five feet, five and a half, four and a half, four feet." I never heard them say "Mark Twain." That must have been reserved for further down the river at Hannibal. When it got to nine, the skipper would slow her down and proceed very carefully. There was no telegraph between the pilothouse and the engine room. In its stead, there was a brass tube with a mouthpiece at each end. The skipper would blow into the mouthpiece causing a whistle at the other end. One of the engineers would put his ear to the tube and the two would carry out their business.

All of the equipment that the district owned had *U.S.E.D.* marked on them. U.S.E.D. stood for United States Engineering Department. That was changed several years later when some Washington bureaucrats objected to the Corps of Engineers calling itself a *Department*. So from that point on all equipment was marked *C.E.*

We lived at 6234 Florence Boulevard next to Miller Park in the northern part of Omaha. This was an upscale part of Omaha at the time. In the winter there was lots of snow and the roads were not cleared all the way down to the pavement. There was always about eight to ten inches of snow and ice. This came in handy because I could put on my ice skates at home, skate three blocks to the frozen pond in Miller Park, and skate home again.

I had my dog, Duke, an Irish setter that had been given to me by our next door neighbor at Fort Scott. The neighbor, a captain named Terry Bull, couldn't take him when he was reassigned. I always wondered what mother would give her son such a name. Anyhow, Duke was mine and was with me all the time. He would walk with me to school every morning, returning home when I entered the schoolhouse. Then at 3:30 in the afternoon he would arrive back to pick me up and walk me home. There was one problem here and that would be when I got sick and couldn't go to school. When my father got home from work he would have to drive to the school and pick up Duke. The school was Minne Lusa Elementary and it is still in business, so I am told. I sent a draft of this vignette to Catharine. I had spelled our school *Minneloos*a, thinking that it was an Indian word like

*Minnehaha*. Catharine informed me that it was two words. Now I wonder who was the prestigious Minne for whom this school was named.

On November 11th at 11:00 o'clock, all classes rose for two minutes of silence and prayer for those who died in WWI. This was Armistice Day and was dedicated to teaching us of the history of this awful war. It was stressed upon us how lucky we were to have been born Americans. We gave the Pledge of Allegiance by placing our right hand over our hearts and then extending it in the direction of the flag when we said *to the flag*. The palms of our hands would face the flag. Later we were told to extend our hand with the palm facing up like we were giving ourselves. This was to differentiate the pledge from the Nazi salute, which had the palm down. Later, extending the arm was eliminated altogether.

In the summer we would go to Fort Omaha to use the swimming pool. With the heat and humidity this would be a must for us kids. It was at the swimming pool that I saw my first West Point cadet. He must have been on the corps swimming team and he was impressive. He was about six feet tall with very broad shoulders, a flat stomach and bulging muscles. He made a racing dive at the end of the pool, just sort of glided to the other end, and effortlessly pulled himself out of the pool. It was at that moment that I decided that I was going to West Point. When he came out of the locker room in his uniform I was hooked.

Another activity that we were able to participate in was horseback riding. Fort Omaha had a stable and several horses. I'm not sure why they still had them in 1936 and what military unit used them. But they needed to be ridden and dependents were encouraged to ride. There was a rather large riding hall that at the time looked to me like it could host a polo game. One Saturday morning Pop packed us all up for a morning of riding instruction. Pop was originally commissioned in the field artillery, and his assignments were with horse drawn artillery. He was a superb horseman, played polo, and had obvious control over any horse he mounted. I was nine years old at the time and my short legs gave me little confidence that I could stay on a horse, much less control one.

All of these military horses were very well trained and knew what they were to do by voice command. Pop stood in the center of the riding hall and the three of us, mounted on our horses and started walking counterclockwise around the hall. Then Pop gave the command "Trot ho" and all three horses would take up a trot. I had yet to master posting and the horse knew it. Then Pop commanded "Gallop ho" and off we went at a gallop. I mostly just hung on with whatever I could find to grab. These weren't western saddles but McClellan saddles, and there was no horn or a sloping backside. From my standpoint, they were more like racing saddles. After one or two laps around the hall, Pop called "Walk ho" and we resumed the slow pace again. My horse had had just about enough of me. I didn't ride like he expected I should, and my lack of posting ability was the breaking point for him. He walked out to where my father was and gently went down on his knees; I stepped off and he rolled all the way over, saddle and all. That was the end of my riding lessons. My next time on a horse was at Boogie's mother's dude ranch in Reno where all the saddles were western saddles.

In 1938 Pop was promoted to captain. He had been commissioned in 1921 and thus had been a lieutenant for seventeen years. The three of us had been trained to answer the telephone in the very proper military way. The phone would ring and whoever was closest would answer "Lieutenant Prentiss's quarters." Most kids of military families did the same, so it just came naturally. Now Pop was promoted and we received instructions that he was now a captain and we had to answer the phone accordingly. The next time I answered the phone I said "Captain Lieutenant Prentiss's quarters." He had been a lieutenant so long I thought it was part of his name. He rose in grade quite rapidly after that to major in 1940, to lieutenant colonel in 1942, and to colonel in 1943. He made brigadier general in 1952 and major general in 1955. Pop retired in 1956 after thirty-five years of active duty.

Most kids like to play games that mimic their father's occupation. After my many trips on the district's riverboats on the Missouri River, I thought it a grand idea to replicate the Missouri River in our back yard. I excavated a meandering river that started at the water faucet and ended at the driveway. I was careful to keep a proper grade so the water would flow. All along the way I constructed levees, training dikes, and sandbars. When I turned on the faucet I had the Missouri River in miniature. Now mind you, this was before the Vicksburg Waterways Experiment Station of the Corps did the same thing for the entire Mississippi River Valley. When my father came home and saw what I had done to the backyard, my days of river modeling came to an end. The next day the yard was returned to its original design. I was told by my mother that this wasn't the only time we three kids played out the part of Pop's occupation. I was born in 1927 when Pop was stationed at Fort Myer, Virginia, right next to Arlington National Cemetery. Pop's unit was a horse unit that was used for the military funerals at Arlington. It seems that my brother, sister, and I would play *funeral*. Eddie and Catharine would roll out the little red wagon and place me in it. This was the caisson and I was the departed veteran. My shoes would be placed on the wagon facing backward and Eddie and Catharine, acting as horses, would pull me around the block while singing "Onward Christian Soldiers."

On Easter of 1937 there was an Easter egg hunt at Fort Omaha. We all went over and participated in a great search for the most eggs. The big guys always won that contest and we little guys got the eggs that been overlooked or refused because the shells had been broken. One very kind mother saw me looking for the leftovers and took me by the hand to a special place. There was a very special egg, a golden one. She said to me to take it to that tall man who was running the show. I did and he made a special announcement that "Happy Prentiss had found the golden egg and had won the special prize, a rabbit." (Only four people call me *Happy* now—my sister, her husband Walt, Tom Loper, and Dave Pettit.) There was a second golden egg, and a girl my age had found it and won a rabbit as well. We took this little bunny home and I named him Poppy. I have no idea how I came up with this name, but he responded to it.

Pop built a cage for Poppy out in the back where the Missouri River had been. Soon Poppy was allowed in the house and became housebroken. When he had to go he would go to the door and thump. We had Duke and a cat, and the three of them got along very well. Poppy particularly liked my mother's dust mop. When Mother brought it out and started on the floors Poppy would hop on the mop for a free ride throughout the house. He also liked to go out to the screened porch where there was a glider. He would get on the glider and get it swinging back and forth as hard as he could get it and then start doing front and back flips.

One day the girl who found the other gold egg asked if I could bring Poppy over to her house to play with her rabbit. It seems that her rabbit was a bit depressed and she thought it might perk it up by playing with Poppy. I did and the two of them had a grand time in the back yard. After about an hour her mother came out and had a fit. It seems that her rabbit was a female. A few weeks later she had lots of bunnies to give away. When we moved to Reno I had to get rid of Poppy. Pop's driver said he would take him. We drove Poppy over to his house and dumped him off. I was sure that Poppy was going to be eaten.

*Sgt. Floyd*

*Sgt. Pryor*

Eddie, Bernie Loper, Catharine, Tom Loper, Me on the *Sgt. Floyd* – 1939

Me, Poppy, Catharine, and Patti Page at Easter egg hunt – 1937

Duke and me – 1937

# Chapter 4 – The Biggest Little City in the World: Reno, Nevada

In 1938 Pop received orders to report to Reno, Nevada, as the regular army instructor to the Nevada and Utah National Guards. When my mother announced this to her ladies' group, one asked, "Who is getting the children?" It seems that back in 1938 in order to get a divorce a couple had to meet state residency requirements, usually at least one year. In Nevada the residency was six weeks. Thus, Reno became the divorce capital of the United States, perhaps the world for all I know. Thus, if someone were to say they were going to Reno it was assumed that it was for a divorce. More than once mother had to set people straight that this was a military—not a personal—move.

Reno, at that time, was the "Biggest Little City in the World." This sign stretched across the main street downtown and it is still there. It was a wide-open western gambling town of twenty-four thousand people from everywhere. Lots of people would come to Reno, get a divorce, and stay. At the front face of the courthouse there were gothic style stone columns that had a ring of lipstick marks all the way around at a height of about five feet. These were caused by grateful divorcees on their way to the bridge over the Truckee River where they would throw their wedding rings into the rushing water below.

My first day at Mt. Rose School was a disaster. School had already started and I was in the fourth grade. I had never owned a pair of long pants for school because Mother didn't think they were practical for rapidly growing

19

boys. My garb was knickers that could start long and by the end of the year still fit. Mother took me to school, Mt. Rose Elementary, and I went through the usual—meeting the principal, checking all of my credentials, being walked down the hall to the fourth grade, and being presented to the class. There were many snickers that I learned later were caused by my wearing knickers. All the boys had on long pants, and all of them were cords. At recess I was *pantsed*, which was a common practice then but I think it has passed away over the generations. When school was over, I left through a different door than the one I had arrived through. I knew the address of our new home, 327 W. Liberty Street and that it was about ten blocks away, but I wasn't sure of the starting direction. Therefore, I walked about ten blocks and kept turning right until I found W. Liberty Street. I had made it through my first day of school in Reno. The next day I wore a pair of cords to school. I haven't worn knickers since, even for golf.

Reno was the ultimate western town with all of the charm of the old west and the glitz of a gambling town. On Saturdays the Indians would come into the town from the reservations and you would see them sitting on street corners. I asked the question one time why the Indians were on reservations and was told because that is where they belonged. At school there was a girl sitting next to me who was Hawaiian—at least that is what she called herself. I don't think she was a real Hawaiian because she could never do the hula even after much begging from her classmates. It was many years later that I learned from one of my black friends that blacks often presented themselves as Hawaiians, who were more acceptable to white society than blacks. When we moved to Washington I was enrolled in Gordon Junior High School. Much to my shock I was seated next to an Indian and I looked around school and saw no "Hawaiians" though there were "Hawaiians" all over Washington. This was difficult for my young mind to rationalize that there was such a difference between the West and the East as to what was considered to be proper associations.

The first week in Reno, my mother was constantly visited by the milkmen. There were three dairies serving Reno, and the milkmen were most anxious to get mother's business. Each would come by and leave a small gift, such as a pound of butter, a dozen eggs, or a bottle of buttermilk. After about a week Mother selected one and he was delighted. He pulled out his pad to get all of the information and started writing: name, address, telephone number, and husband's occupation to which my Mother responded "army". The milkman asked "Salvation?" Now this was during the middle of the Great Depression and the US Army had very little visibility and presence. The army that had lots of visibility and presence was the Salvation Army, so it was a natural mistake for the milkman as well as most of those in Reno.

I liked Reno. There was a lot to do. I had a school friend, Boogie Carmichael or Frasier, whose divorced mother owned a dude ranch. His mother had been married twice and Boogie never figured out which last name to use. She actually married her ranch foreman a little later, so Boogie started using the name Brown. Anyway, Boogie would invite me out to the ranch on weekends. What a blast that was. That was the first and only time I had seen a chicken get its neck wrung and to see a chicken running around without its head. Like everyone else, I had heard these expressions from my mother: "If you don't come over here right now I will wring your neck!" and "You kids quit running around like a chicken with its head cut off!" Now I finally understood the meaning of those expressions. On Sundays, all of the horses were saddled and all of the guests, mostly pre divorcees waiting out their six weeks, went on a twenty-mile breakfast ride into the Sierra Nevada Mountains. We would stop at a little resort place, tie up the horses, and go in for breakfast. What a treat. Every time I hear the song "Sunrise Serenade" by Glenn Miller I am reminded of the breakfast rides because that record was always playing on the jukebox in the restaurant when we arrived.

For two summers, Pop took me to summer camp with him. This was held in Boise, Idaho where the National Guard units from Nevada, Utah, and Idaho would perform their six weeks of active duty. I went as my father's orderly. Since the officer's mess was strictly for officers, my father had to find some way to get me fed. He made arrangements with the company commander of Company C, 116th Engineers, Idaho National Guard, Pocatello, Idaho for me to spend my six weeks with them and to eat at the company mess. This was great. I could get a feel of what the army was all about. Every morning I would get up when the bugle blew, go over to the mess hall for breakfast, and tag along for whatever training was scheduled for the day. I quickly found that this was a gold mine for a collector of insignia. I had started a pretty good collection from stuff my father had given me, but here was a place for good collecting. I begged, bartered, and traded with the troops. I also found that ten cents worth of shoe polish could bring in two dollars. So, I polished shoes and boots for the entire company. On my last day at camp in 1940, the first sergeant came over to our tent with a set of enlisted insignia consisting of a cap insignia, a US and an Engineer Castle with C/116/ID on top. He made me an honorary member of the company. I was delighted and proud, besides being happy to add to my collection. I still have the set in mint condition.

This might have been the end of my relationship with C/116/Idaho NG, but a strange coincidence occurred eighteen years later. I had just returned from a tour in Korea. I reported in to the executive officer of the engineer school at Fort Belvoir for an assignment. He looked at my 201 file and said "Captain Prentiss, you are being assigned to the department of training publications." I said, "Colonel, if there is a choice I would rather be assigned to the Department of Engineering or someplace else where my recent experience as a company commander and battalion operation officer can be used." He said "Nope, you are going over to training pubs. Report to Colonel Klemp, the Director."

Training pubs was considered an absolute dead end assignment. I drove over to training pubs located in an old WWII wooden hospital across US highway 1 from where all of the action was. When I reported to Col. Klemp, he was sitting in his chair with his feet on the desk smoking a rather long cigar. He returned my salute with his cigar between his first and middle finger. He brushed the ashes off his chest as he looked at my 201 file and asked why I was being assigned to training pubs. I responded that I didn't know why. He said that there were two regular army officers assigned to training pubs, he and me. He also let me know that he was the senior colonel, not just at Fort Belvoir but in the whole army and "Look where they put me." He said, "I will let you stick around for about six weeks and then will approve your request for a transfer. I am making you the chief of the field manuals branch. There is a captain down there who ranks you by about four years, but he will report to you. He won't mind."

So, I went over to my new office to meet my staff. Besides the captain, there were four civilian writers and four master sergeants. All of the master sergeants had been officers that had been caught up in a reduction in force. The policy was that unless one could complete twenty years active duty by age fifty-five he was *riffed* but was allowed to stay on active duty at his highest enlisted grade until he completed twenty years active duty. Then he would retire at his highest grade as an officer. One of these master sergeants was Bob Bachman who had been a colonel, commanding an engineer group when he was riffed. One day Sgt. Bachman said something about the 116th Engineers. I perked up and said, "What do you know about the 116th Engineers"? He said the he had entered the army through the Idaho National Guard back in the '30s. I asked what unit he had been in and he said that he was a lieutenant in C Company. I said that I was an honorary member of C Company, that I had attended summer camp with my father the summers of 1939 and 1940. He said "You aren't that little kid that was always in the company area collecting insignia and shining boots are you?" I said, "Yep, that was me."

By the way, the assignment in training pubs was a great one but that is another story.

Pop at summer camp. Boise, Idaho – 1939

Me in front of our tent at National Guard summer camp. Boise, Idaho – 1939

Standing attention
National Guard summer camp. Boise, Idaho – 1939

# Chapter 5 – Back to Fort Belvoir, VA 1941-1944

We arrived in the D.C. area in the summer of 1941. Aunt Margaret had a rental house on T Street that she made available to us as we waited for quarters at Fort Belvoir. Mobilization was in full swing and housing was in short supply. At the end of 1941 we moved into Quarters 31, a group of sixty beautiful brick colonial homes built in 1935 by the Works Progress Administration (WPA). On the 7th of December, 1941, we all went to Griffith Stadium for a Redskins football game against Philadelphia. Around halftime the announcer started asking various public officials to call their office. "Would Senator__ please call your office?" and "Would General__ please contact your office?" My cousin was sitting next to me and said, "There is a war going on some place." When we left the stadium there were newspaper boys selling "extras." The headlines said, "Japs bomb Pearl Harbor." We asked Pop what this meant. His face grew taut and he said we were at war. It was difficult to get back into the gate at Belvoir since there were soldiers deployed all around the post. After being examined several times, we were finally allowed to proceed to our quarters.

The school system in Belvoir was a mess. I had finished 8th grade in Gordon Junior High School in Washington as we were waiting for quarters. The post school went through the 9th grade. Then high school was Western High School in Washington. The Virginia school system would not take the children of the military who lived on post because no Virginia school taxes were paid by the military. So every morning at about 6:30 a military bus would pick us up and drive us into Washington. Washington is a federal city supported by the Congress, so we could attend school there. At 3:30 in the afternoon the bus would pick us up for our return trip to Belvoir. We would get home about 5:00 p.m. If we missed the bus coming home we had to take a streetcar to 12th and Pennsylvania Avenue, get an AB&W bus to Alexandria, and then another AB&W bus to Fort Belvoir. The walk from the Belvoir bus stop to home was about a mile and a half. This meant that we would step inside our houses at about 8:00 p.m. The real down part of all of this was that we military kids were unable to participate in any school sports or other extracurricular activities.

Western High School was rated as the number one high school in the country. It is now called "The Duke Ellington School of The Performing Arts." Pop and Aunt Margaret attended Western. Catharine finished up her last semester there and I spent all three years at Western, graduating in 1945. As WWII progressed, more and more graduates became casualties and their names were posted on the main bulletin board. Several of my classmates dropped out of school and enlisted. As I look at my yearbook every bio had some mention of service—either volunteer work or intentions to enlist. There would be items such as "Molly is a candy striper" and "After his hitch in the merchant marine Jim will enter Princeton." There was real patriotism in the school. On June 6, 1944, D-day in Europe, the whole school was assembled in the auditorium where we were told of the invasion. At the end of the assembly we all bowed our heads as the principal prayed for the safety of our troops. Try that today.

It was sort of tough attending a high school where your father had been top in his class.

Several of my teachers had taught him as well as Aunt Margaret. There was Miss Thompson who taught English, Miss Bass who taught Latin, and Miss McPherson who taught English literature. I was never a very good student and my grades were average. One time in Miss McPherson's class she was returning essays to the class with comments on each as she handed them back. She would say, "Harold, this was very interesting but you had some misspelled words and a few grammatical errors. Please take note." When she came to me she said, "Louis, your father would have never turned in a paper like this." She certainly was correct.

27

Because we who lived at Belvoir could not participate in school activities, we had to find our own. There were no organized kids' activities at Belvoir because there was no manpower to run them. There was no scouting because there were no scout masters available. There was no teen club, teen dances, or teen sports. What we did was to mostly get into trouble, which eventually brought in my father. One day a friend, Charlie Ford, borrowed his father's 12-gauge shotgun and some shells. Charlie and I walked through the woods behind the 1 to 60 housing area to the Potomac River. Belvoir is just downstream from Mt. Vernon. When we got to the riverbank, one of us would throw a can or bottle high in the air and the other would blast it with the 12-gauge. This was sort of unorganized trap shooting. After about fifteen minutes of shooting up all of the shells, we spotted a mounted MP coming down the bridle path. Seeing two armed civilians and suspecting saboteurs, he pulled out his .45, leveled it at us and said, "Drop it and put your hands on your head!" We did, he got off his horse, picked up the shotgun, and marched us in front of him with our hands on our heads all the way to the MP Station. I suspect that he visualized receiving a medal for his capture of not one but two saboteurs. When we got to the MP station the provost martial questioned us and found that Charlie's father was a master sergeant and mine was a colonel. He could find no reason to hold us, so he sent us home after calling our fathers. Charlie's father finally got his shotgun back and my father asked me, "Why do you keep doing things like this that embarrass me?" I had heard this question many times and my answer was always the same: "I didn't think I was doing anything wrong."

One of the things that we kids did was to explore much of what is now considered to be historic. There were sections of trenches that were part of a WWI training area. Only a few of my friends knew where they were, and I doubt that anyone at Belvoir now knows about them. We used to have BB gun fights in the trenches. Shooting at someone's head was off limits, but if you could get him in the butt it was considered a *kill*. Mother used to wonder how I got so many bee stings on my arms.

Along the bluff overlooking the Potomac were the ruins of the old Belvoir mansion. The British destroyed it when they sailed up the Potomac to shell Washington during the War of 1812. The only thing standing now is the foundation and a few sections of walls. One thing that I found—and I suspect no one else knows about—is a two-foot square brick sluiceway that led from the kitchen to the top of the bluff. This was obviously a drain for wash water or anything else that could be washed out from the house. I was exploring around and found a small opening about forty feet from the house. I cleared it and crawled all the way to the ruins. The opening into the house was blocked by rubble. The only thing I found was a broken plate that had a blue design on it. It went into the box of stuff I kept in my room. I also found several lead balls that I would guess to be about a 50-caliber. These may have come from the Civil War or could have been the result of hunting. One day I dragged home two cannon balls that were about the size of a duck pin bowling ball. These stayed on our front yard for about a year until the scrap drive to support the war came to Fort Belvoir. Pop and I each took one and we got our pictures on the front page of the Belvoir newspaper, *The Essayons*, heaving these balls into the scrap pile to help win the war. These cannon balls were obviously from the British assault on Belvoir.

Jack Marvin's father was a battalion commander, and they lived in Quarters 26. Jack was five feet five inches tall and his father was even shorter. The minimum height to pass the West Point physical was five feet six inches. Jack had two years to grow one inch. We were very good friends and did most things together. When it looked like Jack's height was slowing down he decided to do something about it; he decided to get stretched. Once a week for three months we would drive to Baltimore for an appointment with a chiropractor who guaranteed a half inch in three months. Jack was strapped into a duplicate of a medieval rack, his ankles were clamped, there were blocks at his armpits, and his head was strapped to a wheel. For an hour the doctor would gradually crank up the rack. Jack passed the physical and we entered West Point together. I expect that plebe year brought him down to his regular height of five feet five.

Jack was my exploring buddy. Down river from the Belvoir mansion we found a sheer cliff that ran all of the way to the water. There was no way that we could get either up or down without a lot of help. We got a rope, tied it to a tree, and rappelled down the cliff halfway. There we stopped and with my mother's garden trowel we dug a cave. This took us several weeks, but when it was done it was our perfect hideaway. To this day, the only way to get to the cave is by rope. You can't see it from the top of the

# Chapter 6 – First Assignment: Germany 1950 – 1953

WWII had been over for five years and my thoughts of a career in the army were that I would most likely follow the same path as Pop's. All of the captains and above had served in combat and were appropriately decorated. So it was with Pop. He was commissioned in 1921 and wore the WWI Victory Medal for his ROTC service during the war. It would be twenty years before he was awarded another medal, the American Defense Service Medal (The Yellow Jaundice) for service after mobilization but prior to Pearl Harbor. All of us in the class of '50 were awarded the WWII Victory Medal since the war didn't officially end until the end of 1946. I could see a downgrading of the army with promotions very slow. There fortunately seemed to be little chance for a war in the future since the world had exhausted itself with WWII.

I chose field artillery as a branch and Germany as my first assignment. The army had decided that it might be a good idea to send 2nd lieutenants directly to a unit for initial branch training rather than to their basic officers course. This was an experiment to see if the basic course could be eliminated and thus save a few dollars and three months of a lieutenant's career.

We were graduated on June 6th and I became married to Peg on the 8th. That was the first opportunity to book one of the chapels for thirty minutes. Weddings took place every thirty minutes in all chapels from June 6th through June 8th. The reception halls were likewise booked for a one-hour period. Our reception was at Cullum Hall. I had met Peg the summer of '48 at Virginia Beach. Our class was having joint landing maneuvers with the midshipmen from Annapolis at Little Creek, Virginia. We had the weekend off and we all descended on Virginia Beach. Peg and a girlfriend had driven from Bridgeport, Connecticut to spend a week in the sun. They had a transatlantic portable radio with them as they lounged on an oversized beach towel. A classmate and I moved in, attracted by the New England pulchritude and the portable radio. Peg and I swapped addresses and we became pen pals. Christmas of 1949 I gave her a miniature of my class ring and we became engaged.

We had thirty days of graduation leave. The honeymoon consisted of driving around New England in my new 1950 Ford; then we went to Dallas, where Pop was assigned as the division engineer of the South West Division. On June 26th the Korean War broke out and my thoughts of serving in a peacetime army came to an end. Those in my class who were assigned to Japan and Korea had their leave cut short and were shipped to their units, many directly into combat. Those of us who had stateside and European assignments completed our leave and then reported for duty. I reported to New York for shipment to Germany.

We flew to Frankfurt and spent the next few days behind what appeared to be a barbed wire compound. Frankfurt was a mess with bombed out buildings everywhere. The streets were clear, utilities were working, and railroads were moving, but the major reconstruction had not really started. Frankfurt was in good shape compared to Darmstadt and Munich. After a couple of days I received my assignment to the 519th Field Artillery Battalion in Sonthofen in southern Bavaria. There were two major units in Germany at the time, the 1st Infantry Division and the Constabulary. The Constab was organized after the war as an occupation force and was essentially a light armored division. It was a spic and span outfit with highly polished helmets and yellow scarves worn around the neck. No neckties were required.

We left on a train heading south to our first home. As the train rolled through the German countryside we were able to see the immense damage in nearly every town. Also, we could see the intense use of the land. Every patch of farmland was under cultivation and all of the fields were being tended by women. The men were trying to bring in money and the women were bringing in the food.

We arrived in Sonthofen, I called the phone number that was in my orders, and we were picked up by the battalion adjutant who took us up to the kaserne. The Sonthofen Kaserne had been the Hitler Youth School and was now the home of the 36th FA Group and the 519th FA Battalion. After being assigned to a battery we were driven about twenty miles south to Oberstdorf, where all of the family housing was located. The next day we were given the keys to several chalets located above the city in an area called Plattenbitchel. These chalets were all owned by the Nazis who had run the Hitler Youth School in Sonthofen. We picked out a beautiful three-bedroom home just below one of Germany's highest mountains, the Nablehorn. It was fully furnished to include sheets, pillows, pictures, and a maid. I thought of my father's first home in an unfurnished company mess hall at Fort Knox. If army life was going to be anything like the way it was starting, I had made the right choice.

Oberstdorf was at the very southwest tip of Germany, only two miles from the Austrian border. The area had been untouched by the war. The countryside is incredibly beautiful. There was a path that passed our house that let up to the mountain pastures. In the late fall all of the cows were herded down the mountain to their winter quarters. They were brightly decorated and had large bells on their necks that gonged with every step. This procession of musical cows lasted for almost an hour. On the outskirts of Oberstdorf there was a particularly attractive village named Schönblick. I was taken by the view as well as the name, *beautiful view.* Several years later I was sitting with Mother on the porch of her beach house in Delaware and she was talking about how beautiful it was looking over the dunes to the beach and ocean. She said that she needed to name the cottage and asked if I had a suggestion. I told her about the little village in Bavaria named Schönblick. She had me write it down for her but I don't think she ever got around to naming the cottage. In 2005 we bought a condo in Steamboat Springs and named it Schönblick, for the view was similar to the one in Bavaria. There is a carving of the view with its name hanging over the door that Tom Shea did for me.

The next morning I reported to the C Battery Commander, Captain Johnny Golden. He let me know that I was the first officer to arrive in the battalion in about six months. I made the third officer in the battery, the other being a senior 1st lieutenant. I was assigned as the assistant executive officer, the mess officer, the supply officer and the maintenance officer. I collected all of the field manuals I could find to figure out what I was supposed to do. All of this stuff was taught in the branch basic officers' course that we missed.

One day I was sitting in my office reading a manual and Captain Golden called me into his office and asked what the firing battery was doing. I pulled out the training schedule and said, "They are having maintenance." He said, "Do you realize that you should be out there supervising the maintenance?" I said that I did now, saluted, and went out to where the guns were. The 519th was a truck-drawn 155mm-howitzer unit. I had never seen one up close before reporting to the battalion. I spotted the senior NCO, Master Sergeant Konk, who had never returned to the States after the war, had a German girlfriend and several children. A soldier couldn't marry a German at that time. Sgt. Konk was slim, trim, and had a nose like W. C. Fields, big and red. I sided up to Sgt. Konk and asked, "What are they doing at the fifth gun?" He looked down at me rather disdainfully and said, "Do you mean number 5 piece, Lieutenant?" I said, "Yes, number 5 piece." He said, "They are cleaning the equilibrator rods, Lieutenant." I asked "What are they cleaning off the equilibrator rods, Sgt. Konk?" He said, "They are cleaning Cosmoline off the equilibrator rods, Lieutenant." I said "Why is there Cosmoline on the equilibrator rods, Sgt. Konk?' He said, "Number 5 piece just returned from ordinance yesterday and it had Cosmoline on the equilibrator rods, Lieutenant." I learned in this five-minute exchange that senior NCOs—by using one's rank—could avoid using the term *sir* when dealing with a new 2nd lieutenant. After one earned the respect of the troops, *sir* was used.

I took my newfound information about equilibrator rods down to the number 2 piece, looked it over, and found some Cosmoline on the equilibrator rods and promptly called it to the attention of the sergeant in charge. He responded, "We were just getting to it, Lieutenant." I went back to Sgt. Konk and asked, "What are they doing on the number 4 piece?" He said, "They are cleaning the firing vent, Lieutenant." I asked, "What are they cleaning out of the firing vent, Sgt. Konk?" and he replied, "Anything that happens to get into it, Lieutenant." So I went to number 6 piece. This went on until I learned "the maintenance of the piece." It took about a year until I was referred to as *sir*.

The same thing went on in the mess hall, the supply room and the motor pool. I have never felt so bewildered as in my first three months with the 519th. My battery commander knew exactly what was going on and helped me without my knowing. Two weeks after I joined the battery we went to the local firing range for service practice. As I was riding in my jeep I got a call on the radio to move the battery into coordinates (…), lay the battery at azimuth (…) and register it on coordinates (….) I had never seen these weapons fire, much less be responsible for where they fired. I pulled out my field manual, set up the aiming circle (I knew how to do this in Military Topography and Graphics at West Point), laid the battery, and started firing registration rounds. The only comforting thing was that the range was on the upslope of a mountain and you could actually follow the rounds to impact. All of them fell within the range perimeter. I talked about this experience with the battery commander a couple of years later and he said he knew what was going on. He had people watching me. These were gut-wrenching times for this 2nd lieutenant. I was lucky compared to those classmates who went directly to Korea. They had to learn under fire. Thirty-nine of them were killed in Korea, including two of my roommates. Another was severely wounded.

There was a sort of a black market that operated just below the surface. The scarcity of cigarettes and coffee in the German community made them in demand. A carton of cigarettes and a pound of coffee sold for a dollar in the military commissaries. They were worth ten times that amount on the German economy. These were rationed items, but the amounts authorized were well beyond what an individual would reasonably consume. The excess was bartered for things in the German economy. General Lucius Clay was one of the first CINCS in Germany after the war, and his wife established a *barter mart* in Frankfurt where Americans could bring in items that were in excess of their needs, such as cigarettes and coffee, and receive credits that could be used to purchase items that Germans would bring in to sell. Everyone seemed to be happy with the arrangement. One thing that was frowned upon was to sell rationed items for cash. I obtained

Schnipper, a beautiful Dachshund, from a German farmer for a pound of coffee. He was so small that I carried him home in the pocket of my field jacket.

I soon found out that the army wasn't all fun and games. We had a nice house when we could get home. There were battery alerts, battalion alerts, group alerts and 7th Army alerts. These usually started with a phone call about 4 a.m. and required the unit to be packed and on the road in two hours. There was at least one alert per week. In addition, there were spring and fall maneuvers and two weeks every quarter at one of the training areas for firing practice.

There were only two 155mm howitzer battalions in Germany at the time, one in the 1st Infantry Division and the 519th. Our alert position was in the Fulda Gap, which was east of Frankfurt. It took us a twenty-hour forced march to get there. Our battalion had been positioned in Sonthofen for occupation purposes, not for war fighting. We all knew that the Korean War was only a feint for the Russians and that the real war was coming through East Germany. The order came down from 7th Army that we were to move east of Darmstadt to Babenhausen. The kaserne at Babenhausen was occupied by DPs, displaced persons from the war. They were relocated, and the kaserne underwent a major renovation. There was no housing in the area so the families were located to the west of Frankfurt, about an hour's drive to Babenhausen. Because we were so far from the kaserne, only 50 percent of those with families could go home each day and weekend. This—with all of the alerts, maneuvers and trips to the training areas— meant we had even less time at home. Barbara was born in Frankfurt in August of 1951. Peg went into labor on one of the days that I was required to stay in the Kaserne, so a neighbor drove her to the 97th General Hospital where she delivered a few hours later. The next day was my turn to go home, so I drove directly to the hospital to meet my daughter. Still, we in Europe were a lot better off than those in Korea.

Six months prior to my rotation back to the States, the army found that it had a substantial shortage of company grade engineer officers and encouraged officers in other branches to submit a request for transfer. I did, was accepted, and reported to the Engineer School at Fort Belvoir on my return to the States. Again, I was following in the footsteps of my father in that he also transferred from the field artillery to the Corps of Engineers.

Peg at Virginia Beach – 1948

Our first picture, Virginia Beach – 1948

Lt. Jack Baker and me in "Pinks & Greens." Oberstdorf, Germany – 1950

# Chapter 7 – Back to Fort Belvoir, VA 1953-1961

My first assignment in the corps was to the engineer officers' basic course at Fort Belvoir. Our quarters were in the 500 area, which were duplexes that had been divided again into quadroplexes, if there is such a word. I had several classmates there with a former roommate, Lou Genuario, to the left of me, two other classmates up the street, one across the street and yet a fifth to the right. The one on the right, Bob Hughes, had a boxer named Axel, and I had my liver-colored dachshund, Schnipper. Schnipper and Axel were the best of friends, both being imported from Germany, and they would roam the neighborhood together looking for interesting things to do. When there was a strange dog in the area, Schnipper would charge into the stranger, barking his war cry. Axel would be right behind to finish him off. One time I observed this act of teamwork with Schnipper making the charge, but this time Axel's eye caught sight of a new female poodle on the block. So while Schnipper was into the fight of his life, Axel was playing up to the new poodle. When Schnipper looked back and saw no backup he laid on his back with his feet up making an awful wail. The other dog became confused and wondered off.

I spent a year at Belvoir teaching float bridges. This experience would come in handy when I was stationed in Korea.

The summer of '56 I returned to Belvoir to attend the engineer officers' advance course. I don't remember much about this year, particularly what was taught. It was one big year of great social events. John Eisenhower was one of the instructors provided by the infantry branch to teach combined arms tactics. John was a major then and was an excellent instructor. I think that his father being in the White House had something to do with his assignment. There were Secret Service agents outside his house day and night. John and I were selected for promotion to brigadier general on the same orders. He had left the active army and was a member of the reserves. We attended *Charm School* together, an orientation course for newly selected general officers. This was during the Nixon debacle and I asked John what he thought of the situation. His son was married to Nixon's daughter. John said, "He has to go." A couple of weeks later he went.

1959 – 1961: In "Reno" I described the details of my assignment to the Department of Training Publications. I felt that this was certainly the low point in my career and that I probably could never recover from such an assignment. Was I ever wrong? If I had been assigned to the Department of Engineering or any of the other prestigious departments I would have been just another captain. Here in training pubs I was a pearl in the sand. As I have described before, everyone in the department was marking time until retirement. I was the chief of the field manuals branch with the responsibility for the writing of engineer field manuals. I remembered being told at West Point that if you read it in the field manual, it was doctrine. I said to myself, "Prentiss, you are in charge of engineer doctrine." As I looked around training pubs and saw something that I thought should be my responsibility, I would tell that branch chief that I thought this area he was working on should be mine, and he would say, "Sure, take it." In that way, I was able to consolidate all of the doctrinal stuff under my branch. This put me in the spotlight whenever there were doctrinal discussions at the engineer school. For this effort I was awarded the *Green Weenie*—the army commendation medal. After I left Belvoir the army reorganized and consolidated all doctrine under one roof.

I bought a boat and kept it moored on the Potomac below the Officer's Club. It was a beauty, a 33-foot Richardson Sedan made in Tonawanda, New York. This was a classic that you saw in movies of the '30s. I was the third owner. The first was Early Wynn, a famous Washington senator's pitcher who was inducted into the Hall of Fame. The cabin was mahogany bright work, the engine was a Hercules straight six, and it could sleep up to eight. I had an eight-foot sailing dinghy mounted on the roof that I would lower into the water with a swinging davit. I would collect a crew of family or friends on Friday nights after work and sail down the Potomac to its juncture with the Chesapeake Bay. There we would anchor and spend the weekend sailing, fishing, drinking, eating, and telling stories. One of the boat rules was that each person had to take a turn preparing a meal. When one of the civilians in training pubs had his turn for dinner, the salad he prepared was sort of a selection of everything. Someone asked him what he called his salad and he replied, "Surprise salad." When asked what that meant, he said, "Who gets the fishhook?"

The name of my boat was *Marbalynn* which was the combination of my three daughters' names, *Mar*tha-*Ba*rbara-jacque*lynn*. One of the last trips in the *Marbalynn* was with Pop. He owned a cottage south of Rehoboth, Delaware, at Indian Beach. Pop and I decided to sail from Washington to Rehoboth Bay. It was a three-day sail each way and was the last time that I was able to spend some extended quality time with him. Before we docked back at Belvoir he made me shave off my three-day stubble. He was particular with whom he was seen.

The girls swimming in the Potomac near the Chesapeake
Bay. *The Marbalynn* is on the right – 1960

# Chapter 8 – First Tour to the Orient: Korea

You had either been, were going, were going again, or were in Korea in the '50s.

After my transfer to the Corps of Engineers, the army wanted to get me qualified as an engineer officer. I completed the engineer officers' basic course, followed by a year in the Engineer School teaching float bridges, followed by a year in the corps Norfolk district, followed by a year at Princeton University for a master's degree in civil engineering, followed by nine months at the engineer officers' advanced course at the Engineer School. It was time for the army to get some use out of its investment and I was sent to Korea.

I left the family in Stratford, Connecticut with Peg's mother and flew to San Francisco to Honolulu to Wake Island to Formosa to Tokyo to Seoul, Korea. I am not sure how many days it took because we crossed the International Date Line and I completely lost track of both time and date.

I was assigned as company commander of B Company, 76th Engineer Battalion. This assignment was nothing like what I expected. The facilities that US military used in Seoul were those constructed by the Japanese. They had never been modernized or renovated. The army had yet to establish a construction agency in Korea so it had no method of contracting for the modernization of its facilities.

B Company was selected to be this agency. All of the enlisted college graduates in the battalion were assigned to B Company. It was still a conscripted army. The company was organized with the 1st Platoon as the Design and Contract Administration Platoon, the 2nd Platoon as the Inspection Platoon and the 3rd Platoon as the Materials Platoon. We also hired Korean civilian engineers to add to the 1st Platoon. I was given contracting officer authority.

We would be given a group of buildings to be renovated, develop the plans and specifications for the renovation, issue an invitation for bids to the local Korean construction companies, receive bids, and award contracts. Most of the materials used were furnished by the army. The purpose of this program was twofold: to get the facilities modernized quickly and to develop a Korean construction capability. B Company continued to act as a construction agency until the Corps of Engineers established the Far East District.

The rest of the battalion referred to B Company as the *smart company* because we had all of the college grads. Having highly educated soldiers didn't mean that maintaining discipline was easier. In some aspects it was more difficult. The NCOs were not as educated as the soldiers under them. They had more difficulty in gaining their soldiers' respect. The soldiers quickly recognized where the power lay, however.

One day I received a top priority mission to build a double chain link fence around an area for the storage of nuclear weapons. I instructed my platoon leaders to leave only a skeleton crew necessary to manage the contracts and to organize the rest to build the fence.

One of members of the 1st Platoon appeared at my office and asked to speak to me. The first sergeant showed him in. He was one of the "smart" troopers. He said that he had been instructed that he was to be part of a fence building team. I said that that was probably correct. He said that he objected to this assignment because it wasn't part of his MOS (Military Occupation Specialty). I called "first sergeant" and he said "Oh! No, no, no, I have no problems going on the fence detail." The first sergeant came in and I told him that specialist so-and-so said that building a fence was not part of his MOS." The first sergeant said he would explain it to him. When I saw him in the field later that day he understood the priority and importance of the mission.

I had been instructed to do a reconnaissance of the storage site and to lay out the roadway and potential bunker sites. I drove to the site in my jeep and walked up the highest hill and sat down. I spent nearly two hours there, not because I needed the time to complete my reconnaissance but because it was the most peaceful experience I had ever felt. It was warm, there was a slight breeze, and there was nothing man made in view except for the road. To the west I could see the Yellow Sea. They call Korea the "Land of the Morning Calm." I can see why. I have never had that feeling since. After a couple of hours I returned to my jeep. My Korean driver, Kim, asked what I was doing and I told him I was "just thinking."

There were four officers in B Company, three lieutenants and me. Our quarters were in a four-bedroom house just outside the company area. It was complete with a kitchen and a bamboo bar. It was a wet bar with two shelves for glasses. The outside of the bar was faced with two-inch split bamboo running vertically. The four of us would meet regularly after work for a beer and a roundup of the day's activities.

One evening, one of the lieutenants came into the house and laid his belt with holster and .45 Colt automatic on the bar. He was the battalion officer of the day and had just returned from inspecting the troops. I knew that he always kept a round in the chamber of his .45. I was standing behind the bar serving the beer. I served this lieutenant a coke, reached over to his gun belt, pulled out his .45, released the ammunition magazine and cleared the chamber of the round. I left the .45 on the bar top with the slide locked in the open position.

After the lieutenant finished his Coke he put on his belt, slid in the ammunition magazine, let the slide go forward, and pulled the trigger. There was a loud explosion and the sound of broken glass. I looked down on the shelf below me and picked up the .45 slug from the pieces of the broken glass. The slug was directly in front of my stomach. I had heard of stories of the Moros in the Philippines using split bamboo as armor and that it stopped even a .45 slug. The story must be true since the two-inch split bamboo facing on the bar kept the slug from passing through me. After a lecture from me and the two other lieutenants he never carried a round in the chamber again.

Besides our construction responsibilities the battalion had contingency missions in case the "balloon went up." One task was to build a float bridge over the Han River. Because I had taught float bridging at the Engineer School, the battalion commander selected me to be the bridge commander. Normally he would direct this mission himself because it involved the assets of the entire battalion. I did a reconnaissance of the area and selected A Company to install the anchorage system, B Company to erect the bridge and C Company to build.

There were many orphanages in Korea as a result of the war. My company decided that it wanted to sponsor one, the Yong Nac Orphanage. This was sort of a two way street; the orphanage would get much needed support from us, and the troops in the company would have an opportunity to escape army life by spending some free time with some loving children. The first thing that the orphanage needed was clothing. The troops sent letters home asking for donations of used clothing to be sent to the company. In order to clear the postal services, the packages were to be addressed to *Orphanage Fund* in care of the name of the trooper. In a couple of weeks the response was incredible. We received so many boxes that they filled up the mailroom and an adjacent building. The amount of clothing was well beyond the needs of the orphanage so we asked them to share with other orphanages. I had one trooper come up to me asking if a package had come in for him. I told him that I had no idea because as quickly as we could they were given to the orphanage. He said that his package really wasn't supposed to go to the orphanage in that he had something sent for his Korean girlfriend. He had used the Orphanage Fund address to "expedite" it. I often wondered what the orphanage did with a size 6 flimsy nightgown.

One Saturday I drove to the orphanage and brought one of the children back to the company to spend the day. I brought her up to the officer's quarters and all of us had a ball trying to teach each other Korean and English. She asked for *mul* and none of us had any idea what that was. I called up to the headquarters and asked one of the Korean interpreters what mul was. She said "Captain, you have a woman up there, don't you?" I said "Yes, and she is four years old." She told me mul was water, so we gave little Kim a drink. Later in the year I went on R&R to Japan and asked the director of the orphanage if there was something I could bring back for them. He asked for three knitting machines. These were remarkable. All that was needed was to thread the machines with yarn, set some controls, and then push a handle back and forth until the proper length was achieved. I brought them three and they were delighted. Just prior to my return to the States the director came out to see me with knitted pants and sweaters for all three of my girls.

The army was building up its presence in Seoul. Dependents were now being authorized, and so facilities oriented toward dependents were being planned. The area where the 76th Engineer Battalion was located was designated to be a dependent area with schools and a commissary. We were instructed to move from Seoul to an area near the end of the runway at Kempo Airfield, about thirty miles south of Seoul. The battalion had also received another high priority assignment, the construction of an eighteen-hole golf course. The battalion commander assigned the operations officer (S-3) as the "Golf Course Project Officer."

This move required the battalion commander to fill the operations officer slot, a major's position. I was the junior captain in the battalion but the only one with a graduate degree in engineering. He selected me to fill this slot.

The move required the battalion to design and build permanent facilities. My new office did all of the site planning as well as the design for utilities, roads, barracks, mess halls, latrines, BOQs, maintenance facilities, and the headquarters. This was real engineering. As quickly as I could finish a portion of the plans, one of the companies would take on the work. We accomplished building our new area and moved into our new home before my fifteen-month tour ended. I kept a copy of each plan that I had signed and used it as an example of engineering experience when I applied for registration as a professional engineer in the District of Columbia.

Rather than fly home I requested, and it was approved, to return by ship. This had three advantages over flying: one was being able to catch up on some rest, one was able to take advantage of the great food and fun and games that the ship provided, and one's rotation date was calculated from the date of departure from the United States to the date of arrival back. Thus I was able to leave Korea about fourteen days earlier than if I had flown. I was ready. The ship was the USAT General Daniel I. Sultan. Five years later my whole family would sail from New York on the same ship when we went to Peru.

Four members of the Yong Nac Orphanage. Kim is on the right – 1956

The New Battalion Home: Kempo, Korea – 1956

Comments

# Chapter 9 – My Favorite Assignment: Peru

About three months prior to graduation at the Command and General Staff College (C&GSC) at Fort Leavenworth we were all given preference cards to be filled out indicating our desire for the next assignment. These cards helped the personnel types put you where you wanted to go as best they could. You filled them out with first, second, and third choices for both the type of assignment and location. We always considered this sort of a sham because there were nine different options that could be made, so the Per guys could always say, "You got what you asked for" even if they gave one number three for type assignment and number three for location. I did a mental evaluation of my career and concluded that since I had served as a company commander, a battalion operation officer, a construction project manager and the executive officer in an engineer district, the other two fields in the Corps of Engineers that would round out my career were facilities maintenance and topography. I wasn't interested in being a post engineer, so I chose topography as the type of assignment. As far as location was concerned, I thought it would be fun to be in Latin America where I could use my limited Spanish. To the personal types this was like two straight lines crossing. Topo and Latin America meant The Inter American Geodetic Survey (IAGS). I had never heard of IAGS and knew nothing about Topo except what was taught on the top floor of Washington Hall at West Point, Military Topography and Graphics (MT&G). My assignment came ordering me to Lima, Peru as the Officer in Charge of the Peru project, IAGS. I didn't know then that a Topo assignment was, like training pubs, a career kiss of death. Most of the rest of the class got orders to Vietnam as advisers to the Vietnamese army.

Prior to my travel to Lima, I attended a three-week blitz course in Spanish at the Sanz School of Language in Washington, D.C. My folks lived in Washington, so we stayed there while I attended school. I never expected what I got into. This blitz course was six hours a day, six days a week with one instructor teaching one student. My teacher was from Argentina and her husband was in their embassy. From the start all conversations were in Spanish. English was used only as the last resort when there was no other way to communicate. A typical day started with the normal greetings and then the questions started, all in Spanish:

Q. What did you do today?
A. I had breakfast and drove down here for class.
Q. Hadn't you gone to bed last night?
A. Yes.
Q. How did you eat breakfast and drive the car when you were still in bed?
A. I got up out of bed, had breakfast and drove here for class.
Q. Didn't you go to the bathroom, clean up and dress?
A. Yes, I got up, went to the bathroom, cleaned up and dressed prior to eating breakfast and driving here to class.
Q. How did you clean up?
A. I showered, shaved, brushed my teeth, and combed my hair and then dressed.

By this time it was noon and a break for lunch. In the afternoon we went through everything I had for breakfast as well as how I ate it, cutting the eggs, buttering the toast putting cream in the coffee, and wiping my mouth with the napkin. This was just day one. In the days to come she learned all about my family, where I had lived and what my likes and dislikes were. What a great spot for a secret agent to fill up a dossier on someone. In two days I was dreaming in Spanish.

We drove from Washington to New York where I took the car to the terminal for shipment to Lima and we boarded an army transport ship for the Canal Zone. We stopped in Guantanamo where some troops were off-loaded and some troops were on-loaded. When we reached the Canal Zone we loaded into a Braniff Airlines flight for Lima.

The family arrived and was picked up by Jack and Mary Ella Waggener. Jack was a friend and fellow engineer officer; he was in the class of '48 at West Point, the same as Walt's class. Jack was the engineer member of the army mission in Peru. After a couple of days with the Waggeners we moved into a pensión as we waited the arrival of our household goods and to find a place to rent. We ended up spending six weeks in the pensión. The first evening meal was an interesting one for the family. We were served family style with each family seated at separate tables. At each place there was an artichoke. The girls had never seen an artichoke. Here was this grey green thing with prickly leaves in front of them that they were supposed to eat. I looked into these bewildered faces and decided to set up some rules. They went like this: "We are going to be here in Peru for three years and we are going to run into many foods that we have never seen or tasted. Rule one is every time there is a new food served we all must eat one full serving. Rule two is that if you don't like the food after eating a full serving you don't have to eat it again." They all agreed that this was fair and would comply. As a result they enjoyed and ate everything.

The first morning we sat down to a typical continental breakfast. The girls saw some boxes of dry cereal on a corner table and asked me if they could have some. I knew the words for wheat and corn but not for cereal. I called the waiter over and asked in Spanish, "What do you call that over there?" pointing to the boxes. He responded, "Corn flakes." What a way to deflate one's ego when he is trying to impress his daughters with his Spanish capability. I found out that there are lots of English words that are generic words in Spanish. *Corn flakes* meant any type of dry cereal. This came up again after we had moved into our house. We had a houseboy who was responsible for the upkeep of the outside of the house, including washing the car. Juan came to me one day asking for what sounded like a "he leta." He was washing windows and wanted a "he leta." When he saw I didn't understand he said "para afeitarse" (to shave yourself with). What he was asking for was a razor blade to scrape some paint off the window. Gillette has become a generic name for a razor blade and is pronounced *jiletta*.

In my thirty one years in the army I consider my assignment to Peru to be the most interesting, challenging, and rewarding. IAGS was established after WWII to tie the North and South American continents together and to create topographical maps. The army found during WWII that navigational aids, maps, and precise geographic locations were woefully inadequate in Central and South America. It established bi-lateral agreements with nearly every country in central and South America to fix the problem, Argentina being one of the exceptions. The program, probably the most effective foreign assistance program ever, was very simple. The United States would provide the funds, the expertise, the equipment, the material, and the training to the host country so that it could perform a programmed geodetic and topographic survey of its country. In the case of Peru we equipped and trained the army's Military Geographic Institute, the Navy's Hydrographic Institute and the Air Force's National Aerial Photographic Service. All work was accomplished in duplicate, the host country getting one copy and the United States getting the other. I had in my office an executive officer, six professional civilians (cartographers, topographer, surveyors, etc.), a supply sergeant, about twenty-five Peruvian nationals, a motor pool with thirty or so vehicles, and an air section with a DeHaviland Otter, an L-19 reconnaissance fixed wing, and two H-23L supercharged helicopters. The air section was manned with four pilots and two crew chiefs.

IAGS headquarters was in the Canal Zone. I had never met my boss or been to the headquarters. After about four months my boss, Colonel Unverfurth, wrote me and said that it was about time that he met me and for me to get an orientation. I flew up to the Canal Zone to start my orientation. The first night that I was there I started feeling bad. I was in the BOQ and alone. I started getting the chills and a fever. I walked over to the dispensary and saw a medic. He said it looked like the flu and gave me some APC's. The next morning Colonel Unverfurth had me picked up and I started my orientation. By ten o'clock I was feeling so bad that I told Colonel Unverfurth I had to go to the hospital. The doctor took one look at me and admitted me with viral pneumonia. My temperature quickly rose to 105 degrees and I went into uncontrollable shakes. This was the first and only time in my life that I thought I was going to die. A nurse would strip me and pour a bottle of alcohol on me. This caused my temperature to drop temporarily but the shivering to increase. The swing of my temperature and the alcohol rubs continued for two days. On the third day my temperature dropped and stayed down. My boss said that he and several others had come to visit but I never remembered their being there. I think that I must have gone into a coma. After three days I saw that I had a roommate. He was a Panamanian newspaper publisher who had been president of the Republic of Panama. He was a most interesting man to talk to about his experiences being president. I asked him if he was still active in politics and he said the most profound statement I think I have ever heard: "No, I am no longer in politics. I just want to control the politicians."

The girls got all screwed up in school. Since Lima is in the southern hemisphere, its school year begins in March and ends in December. Marti had just started first grade in Washington when I was going to Sanz School of Languages. We arrived in Lima at the end of September so she was placed in the first grade and was promoted to the second grade after only ten weeks of school. Jacque did the same thing in third grade and Barbara the sixth. They all got reversed when we returned home and ended up at the proper grade for their age. All three became quite proficient in Spanish.

I have always had fun talking geography with my friends. It is amazing how little the typical American knows about South America. I would ask such questions as: What is the elevation of Lima? Lima is due south of what American major city? What is the size of Peru compared to one of our states? Rarely would a person get even one correct.

I had a great opportunity to spend some time in the Amazon jungle. A Peruvian friend, Pepe Lazarraga, was the Director of the Peruvian National Office for the Evaluation of Natural Resources. I had set up a program with his office to assist him, similar to the mapping and surveying program with the Armed Forces. This program was funded by the Agency for International Development (AID). I got three civilians added to my staff— an agronomist, a forester, and a geologist. Pepe asked me to accompany him on a trip into the jungle. Lima is on the coast due south of New York City. To get to the jungle by land, we needed to drive on dirt roads over the Andes, across the high plain, over the eastern ridge of the Andes into the rainforest. We did this in an International Carryall. A driver returned the car back to Lima. Peru is a large country—twice the size of Texas— and has a varied geography. The coast is desert, the Andes are amongst the highest mountains in the world (over twenty-four thousand feet), and the jungle is one of the densest in the world. The pass we took over the mountains was at sixteen thousand feet. You need an oxygen bottle at this

55

height. We drove to Pucallpa, a little Indian village on the Ucayali River. Here we boarded a twenty-four-foot inboard/outboard fiberglass boat making its maiden cruise. The twin I/O's had been hooked up in reverse so that when the steering wheel was turned to the right the boat would turn to the left. They didn't have the right tools to correct the problem. After a couple of days the operator got the hang of it and had no problems. In short, what we did was to sail down the Ucayali over a thousand miles to the Peruvian city of Iquitos. From there we took an airplane back to Lima. In between was a wonderful adventure. The Ucayali flows from south to north. It meets the Maranon (the first *n* is pronounced like a *y*) River, which flows from west to east. At this point the river is about a mile wide and is considered to be the Amazon River by many. From the Maranon, it's another one hundred miles and you reach Iquitos. Iquitos is an Atlantic Ocean seaport. The Amazon is tidal at Iquitos and flows 3,500 miles to the Atlantic Ocean. There is a substantial plywood industry here and freighters sail up the Amazon to Iquitos as a port of call. It took us about ten days to make our jungle trip. In 1941 Peru and Ecuador went to war over a border dispute. Peru loaded its army on ships and sent them through the Panama Canal up the Amazon River to Iquitos to fight the Ecuadorians.

Sailing the Ucayali was like being the first explorers. It was virgin country with triple canopy jungle on both sides. The banks of the river swarmed with creatures of all sorts. There were monkeys, crocodiles and birds of every size, shape, and color. We met only one group of Indians. They were on the bank next to a small creek flowing into the river. They had dugouts, fishing nets, spears, bows, and arrows. We pulled over to the bank and were invited to participate in their fishing. They would pull a dugout up stream about four hundred yards and push off into this rather swift creek. Then they would cast their nets, float down to the river, and haul in their nets. The fish they caught were substantial in number, size, and variety. The most amazing thing to me was that they were large tropical fish. These were large examples of those little ones that we keep in an aquarium like angelfish. The Indians dressed the fish, built a fire, wrapped the fish in banana leaves and placed them in the fire. They also had platinos (plantains) that look like bananas but need to be cooked; they tossed those into the fire as well. After a bit they pulled them out and we ate angelfish. The only other people we met were at a small village on a tributary about a half-mile off the river. It was populated by Japanese who had immigrated to Peru after WWII. We had a dinner of fried pork liver and it was delicious. We had no maps of the jungle, so we navigated the river by taking the largest branch. When my pilots flew over the jungle they always made a detailed flight plan and always followed a river. If they went down we knew they would be on a bank somewhere.

One day at the office I decided that I wanted to learn to play the guitar. I asked my Peruvian secretary if she knew of a guitar instructor. She did and said she would have him come over to my house. This was great and I had visions of my being able to play like the Beatles or Willie Nelson. The next day my instructor showed up—another *Pepe*. (Pepe is a nickname for Jose.) He had a nylon string guitar with him for me to use. He started out with the basics of how to string it, tune it, hold it, and finally, how to strum and pick it. After this first lesson I realized that I wasn't going to be a Willie Nelson but a Segovia. He was going to teach me how to play a flamenco guitar. I took lessons twice a week for nearly three years and enjoyed playing immensely. When I opened my guitar case after we returned home I found that the change in humidity had caused my beautiful guitar to crack and warp such that it was unplayable. I never found another that I could play as well.

One Friday evening we were invited to dinner across the street. After we had finished eating there was a phone call. The host answered and came to me saying the ambassador wanted to talk with me. I answered and he said that it was reported that one of my aircraft, the *Otter*, had crashed and that the pilot and a crew chief had been killed. They had been identified and he gave me their names. The embassy had requested my office to assist in the search for a prominent Peruvian official whose helicopter was missing in the jungle. I had the most difficult job of informing two wives that their husbands were dead. I knocked on the door of the pilot's home and was greeted by his surprised wife who said, "What in the world brings you here at this time of the night, or has something happened to Dick?" After I told her what I knew I looked up the stairs to my left and saw his three young kids sitting at the top wide eyed in disbelief. The wife of the other pilot in the field came over and spent the remainder of the night with her. I left to see the crew chief's wife and three children. This was the most difficult night I have ever spent. Years later in Germany I had to tell one of my civilian employees that his son had been drowned in Italy in a scouting trip. Awful responsibilities!

We lived down the street from a Peruvian professor, Fernando Beleunde Terry. Peru had gone through a series of military coups and was emerging out on the last with free elections and Beleunde was one of the candidates. He heard of the work we were doing and asked to be briefed. His interest was the economic development of the eastern part of the country. Over half of the population of the country lived above 12,000 feet and were essentially out of the economy of the country. The biggest problem was a complete lack of communications. His idea was to construct what he called "La Carretera Nacional de la Seja de la Selva," the National Highway along the eyebrow of the Jungle. We briefed him in Spanish on our entire program. He was particularly interested in the progress of our mapping. We were mapping at both 1/25,000 and 1/100,000 scales. He thanked us and asked if we could brief him in the future. We of course said yes. Beleunde was elected and moved into the presidential palace. After he was in office for about a month I received a call saying that the president wished an update on the mapping program and asked that I come to the presidential office. This went on for two years. I would report all of this at the ambassador's weekly country team meetings. One time he said, "Major Prentiss, you see the president more than I." After I left Peru there was another military coup, and Beleunde came to the United States to become a professor at Johns Hopkins University in Baltimore.

The senior US military commander in Latin America was the CINC southern command. When I was in Peru he was a four-star general named O'Meara. He was a stuffed shirt, pompous individual who also was a bully. General O'Meara would make periodic visits to each country and receive briefings. I was asked to brief him on our program. The briefings were held in the embassy and members of the army mission briefed first. General O'Meara ripped into each briefer: "Where did you get that information? It's wrong and you should know better. You don't know what you are talking about. Sit down. I don't want to hear any more from you." All of these officers were quite competent but not prepared to be bullied by a four-star general. My turn was next. The previous briefers had their stuff on slides using an overhead projector. Mine was on an easel and consisted of a base map and four overlaying transparencies. I was showing the status of the geodetic survey, topographic survey, cartographic mapping, and aerial photography. My point was that we were running out of the aerial photography that would hold up the rest of the work. I wanted him to get the Air Force to take some more pictures. I set up my easel about six feet from him and General O'Mara leaned forward in his chair squinting. He had been used to the overhead projector and wanted me to realize that my training aid was not up to par. I picked up the easel and plopped it down two feet from his face. He pulled back and said, "What is that red area on the map?" I explained that it was the Department of Laredo and he said, "The hell it is." I said, "It is, General. However, the colors on this base map are irrelevant to the briefing." I finished my briefing without further interruption, asked if there were any questions, and took my easel to the rear of the room. His aide-de-camp came over to me and said "Congratulations. No one has ever stood up to the hard-hearted bastard." We did get the Air Force back down to Peru the next summer.

I returned to the States in 1965 to attend the Armed Forces Staff College. After a month of classes I was told to report to the commandant's office where I was presented with the Legion of Merit, an honor at that time reserved for colonels and retiring brigadier generals, not for majors. Maybe General O'Mara's heart had softened a bit.

Visit the following site for an interesting video titled "Mapping Adventure." It is all about IAGS, mostly Peru: www.youtube.com/watch?v=TGY65o3Mm2W

Ken Rinehart, Col. Montezuma, Capt. Zimmic, Col. Unverfurth, MG Paraud, Me. Col. Unverfurth had just received a decoration and silver tray from the three Peruvians who headed the three military mapping agencies. Lima, Peru – 1963

Netting tropical fish on inlet to the Ucayali River – 1964

Lunch of fish and platino – 1964

Aviation section in the field – 1963

Davy Byars, Marti, Barb, Jacque on the way to school – 1962

Comments

# Chapter 10 – Back to the Orient: Vietnam

Since the District of Columbia was established, it was governed by a three-person Commission appointed by the president. Pop was appointed by President Truman to be the Engineer commissioner in 1952. The engineer commissioner was a Corps of Engineers Brigadier General, and he authorized three Corps of Engineers lieutenant colonels as assistant engineer commissioners. In 1965 I was assigned to the District of Columbia as the assistant engineer commissioner for Community Renewal. There was a concerted effort by the population of the district to change the form of government to an elected type. On the recommendation of the president and the concurrence of both Houses of Congress the government changed; I was fired and ordered to Vietnam.

My reporting date for movement was January 10, 1967. I said good-bye to the family and flew out of Dulles to San Francisco. On this flight I saw something I don't think I will ever see again. The ground was covered with snow from Washington to California. Only the last portion of the flight into San Francisco was there some green. From Oakland I flew on a chartered jet to Hawaii, to Guam, and then to Saigon. It was a very comfortable flight with great meals and friendly stewardesses. They played around with the troops, and they loved it. As we were coming into Saigon the atmosphere changed and the stewardesses stopped their playing around, became serious and very professional. They were making this flight on a regular basis, and they knew that many on the flight would be killed or wounded. As we disembarked they had watery eyes.

We arrived late in the afternoon, and I was taken to a B.O.Q. and shown where the mess hall was. My wristwatch shot craps a week earlier, and I had decided to buy a new one when I arrived in Vietnam. My first night in the country was pretty difficult. I was suffering from jet lag big time, and I had no idea what time it was. There was no clock or radio in the B.O.Q. I went to bed when it grew dark and fell fast asleep only to be awakened by the sound of eight-inch howitzer fire. This intermittent fire continued all through the night. The battery was no further than two hundred yards from the B.O.Q. The next morning I got up when the sun came up, had breakfast, and waited to be picked up to go somewhere.

After about an hour a jeep picked me up and drove me to U.S. Army Viet Nam (USARV) Headquarters where I was escorted into the office of the senior engineer in Vietnam, MG Charlie Duke. Gen Duke had been the engineer commissioner for the District of Columbia when I was assigned as one of his assistants. He greeted and welcomed me to Vietnam. After some chit chat he asked me what I wanted to do. I responded what I really wanted to do was to command a battalion. He called in his executive officer and asked when the next battalion command was coming up. The exec responded that the next command would be the 169th Engineer Battalion in two months. General Duke said, "Give the current commander an early drop. I am sending Lt. Col. Prentiss down to the 169th. He called BG Chapman, the CG of the 20th Engineer Brigade telling him that I was on my way to Long Binh to take command of the 169th Engineer Battalion. The 159th group commander, Colonel "Tom" Jones was also informed of this change in command. This is not the way personnel matters were usually handled. Bill Wray, the current commander, was understandably upset because he wanted to complete his command tour. I was under a lot of pressure to produce because of the perceived command influence in my selection for command.

A couple of weeks after I took command TET started. We were put on added alert and doubled to the number of men in the perimeter bunkers. At about 6:00 a.m. on the second day of the TET offensive, the local ammunition bunker was blown up. I was in a mess hall when it blew, nearly ripping off the roof of the mess hall. Scrambled eggs flew everywhere as the troop sought cover. I didn't realize that TET was anything out of the ordinary. I thought this was normal and would be this way for my next twelve months. One thing I noticed, and this may be true of other wars, was that some troops intentionally put themselves in harm's way either to get a medal or an early drop home being wounded. I know of one officer who I suspect intentionally cut his leg with a piece of broken glass so as to claim a Purple Heart.

The battalion had construction missions all over the southern part of Vietnam. Many of the missions were opening up roads, both for military purposes and as part of the pacification program. We rebuilt and paved roads, put in drainage systems, and built permanent bridges. One day I was doing a reconnaissance of a road and suddenly got a feeling that said *stop*. I had my driver pull over, and we just sat there. About twenty minutes later a civilian van came roaring down the road pretty badly shot up with several passengers wounded. They had been ambushed about a half-mile down the road. There was something there looking over me to cause me to stop the jeep.

One of the most unusual missions we got was to de-water a small village that had been bombed by mistake by an Air Force B-52. These types of raids were incredible. One could not see the planes as they flew over. Suddenly the ground would erupt with endless explosions. The raid on this village was tragic. The town was considered to be very friendly and politically it was important to help them to get back on their feet. I flew in by helicopter and saw that the entire village was under water. The chopper hovered as I stepped into waist- deep water. All of the dikes protecting the village had been breached by bombs. The river that ran through the village was tidal, so every twelve hours it flooded. I brought in some float bridging to make a raft, brought in a crane with a drag line, and set up a dredging operation to rebuild the dikes. This worked well for a few days, and we were slowly keeping the river out of the village until the Air Force did another B-52 raid a couple of miles away. The vibrations caused by the bombs triggered mudslides on the recently rebuilt dikes causing them to slough and thus to fail. My next attempt was to have the villagers weave bamboo cribs that I then filled with the dredged material. This worked, and we were able to pump the village dry.

The last time I flew into the site there were two body bags by the helipad waiting for evacuation. We were being protected by an infantry company, and they had lost two men by drowning. When I was in the airport in Saigon waiting for my flight home I picked up a discarded newspaper from Wheeling, West Virginia. In it was a story about a local soldier who had been drowned near the same village we were helping. He was one of the two who were next to the helipad.

After six months in command of the 169th, General Chapman brought me up to the brigade headquarters as the chief of operations (CHOPS). I always liked to sound of being called the CHOPS. There were three engineer groups in the brigade and seven engineer battalions in each group. The main responsibilities of the CHOPS were to assign tasks to the groups and to reallocate assets. This was a very interesting change for me in that I was in a position to see a much broader picture of what was going on. I was the main eyes and ears for the brigade commander and as such was required to spend much time in helicopters visiting operational sites. As could be expected, with many hours flying one got into predicaments. I crashed and burned in one, was shot at with an RPG just missing the helicopter by inches, got shot down by a 50-caliber machinegun, went down in the delta with an engine fire, and nearly crashed when the helicopter's skid snagged on a roll of concertina wire. It seemed that every time I took a helicopter something happened. It got so that every time I showed up the helicopter crews cringed.

Half way through my tour I went on R & R to Hawaii. Peg met me there, and we spent seven wonderful days together. This is the only time in my life I have ever felt rich. I had a roll of $20 bills in my pocket. I had heard an expression that you are rich when you have $1 more than you need to spend. That was my position. Whatever we wanted to do we could afford. Saying good-bye and flying off in opposite directions was difficult. I think that unaccompanied tours for the military are much harder on the families than the soldier.

After six more months in country it was time to rotate back to the States. I flew out of Saigon to Oakland. After processing, I was driven to the San Francisco International Airport. I had about a two-hour wait for my plane to Dulles. There was spray-canned graffiti throughout the airport. The peace symbol was everywhere. I was in a rather wrinkled uniform from the long trip. I was sitting in a chair reading a magazine when a couple of ragged hippies came up in front of me and started yelling "Look at the f—ing hero. Look at all of his ribbons. How many people did you have to kill to get those medals?" I looked back to my magazine and kept reading and they finally left. What a welcome back from the war by what I refer to as *society's sycophants.*

The flight to Dulles was an overnight one and uneventful. We landed at about 6:30 in the morning. There was no one in the airport that I recognized. I got my luggage and sat down and waited. After about a half hour both my mother and father arrived. When Pop saw me he started yelling "My son, my son." I had never seen him so emotional. A few minutes later Peg and the girls arrived and we went home. Here was the real homecoming. Barbara told me a few years later that when she said good-bye when I had left for Vietnam that she never thought she would see me again. With all of the stuff on TV at the time, the only returning soldiers shown were dead ones. That is what she expected.

Bombed village north of Saigon – 1967

Helicopter crash, Ides of March – 1967

Survivors of a helicopter crash, March 15, 1967. Col Jones, BG
Chapman, CSM Van Autreve, Capt Brady, Me, CSM Vernon

## Comments

# Chapter 11 – Edgar Allen Poe's Baltimore, MD

Herb Haar was the district engineer of the New Orleans District when I was attending the National War College. I had known Herb since the '40s. He was a native Virginian, had gone to VPI, and had dated Catharine briefly. Herb wrote to me saying that he was retiring and that if I wanted a really good job after War College, to tell them that I wanted the New Orleans District. I did, but was told that the Chief of Engineers, LTG Clark, said that the only place Prentiss was going was to the Baltimore District. I had followed Herb as the assistant engineer commissioner for the District of Columbia, and as such had been involved with planning and construction in metropolitan Washington. So it was that in 1972 I moved the family to Arnold, Maryland, a small town near Annapolis. The commute to Baltimore was about forty-five minutes. The Baltimore district was one of the largest districts in the corps. It had the military construction responsibility in seven states for the army and the air force, and the civil works responsibility in parts of five states. The construction workload in the Baltimore district was the largest in the corps.

When I think of memories of my time in Baltimore, I think of Flood Agnes. Everything else is insignificant in comparison. In mid-June of 1972, Agnes, a minimum hurricane, spun out of the Yucatan Peninsula into the Gulf of Mexico, crossed the Florida panhandle and the southern states into the Atlantic. The winds decreased to a tropical storm. It swung back into the east coast dumping very heavy rains from Virginia to New England. Damage from winds was minimal, but flooding was widespread from Virginia to the southern part of New York. At the time, Flood Agnes was the most costly natural disaster the country had ever faced, estimated at $3.1 billion. Although the loss of life was not as great as with other storms—117 deaths—the damage was widespread and substantial. The Baltimore District's Civil Works area of responsibility was defined by watersheds. It included the Shenandoah River, Potomac River, the Chesapeake Bay and all rivers flowing into it, with the Susquehanna being the most significant. In essence, in the course of two days, the entire district area of Civil Works responsibility was under water. The roads were closed to Baltimore so I drove to Fort McHenry, had one of the district's boats pick me up and bring me to Baltimore. My driver met me and I spent the next six weeks living in Baltimore.

I remembered a story that my father had told me about the big flood in New England a few years prior to Agnes. General Pick was the chief of engineers at the time and he flew up to Boston where he was met by the New England division engineer. The division engineer gave a briefing on the status of the flood fight and stressed the fact that public relations were under control, that he had PR people at all of these locations, and that he wanted to insure the chief that there would not be any bad publicity. General Pick relieved him on the spot and immediately dispatched another officer to take his place. His priorities were inverted. If he had focused on fighting the flood, the PR would take care if itself. As the waters from Flood Agnes were still rising, I started organizing area offices manned by my office staff. It was clear that I didn't have enough capability to do what was necessary so I asked the chief's office for help. I received nearly one hundred civilian professionals from other districts as well as several officers from the Engineer Officer Advance Course at Fort Belvoir. I brought them into the conference room, briefed them on the situation as best we knew, and appointed each captain as an area engineer. I gave each contracting officer authority for unlimited contracts up to $50,000, a duffel bag containing manuals, forms and office supplies, and the keys to a rental truck; then I told them all to go find a place and solve the problem.

This approach worked. Bedford Forrest said, "Get there firstest with the mostest." This was sound advice. Area offices were set up in motels, hotels, courthouses, and office buildings. The very fact that we were in place with a capability to do something made us successful. We also had the big key—money—and the authority to spend it. General Lincoln was the director of the Office of Emergency Management which operated out of the White House (now called the Department of Homeland Security.) He told General Clark, "You have the keys to the Treasury—just get the job done." Because we were there "firstest with the moistest," our area offices became the focal point for the flood fight and later for the disaster recovery phase. The Red Cross, the National Guards, Housing and Urban Development officials, and various state agencies all set up shop either with us or next to us. Coordination was simple. We mobilized the entire construction industry in the affected areas and put it to work. All contracts were negotiated. In a six week period we had written over 3,600 contracts. I told my comptroller that I wanted each invoice paid within seventy-two hours after its submittal by a contractor. He said, "Colonel, we can't do that." I said, "Then I'll find a comptroller who can." He got the message and we started paying in seventy-two hours. A remarkable thing occurred as a result of this policy. The cost of contracts nearly halved when contractors found that they didn't have to use their funds or borrow to cover their operational costs. When everything was done we bundled up all of the files and released all of our borrowed help. Out of 3,600 contracts we had zero disputes or claims.

I have always been a coin collector and was well into it when I went to Baltimore. I needed something to reward all of the folks who participated in the Flood Agnes disaster. I had a special coin minted as an Agnes commemorative coin. I gave them out and told everyone who helped to carry it as a reminder of their outstanding accomplishments. A couple of years later I saw that various army units were having unit coins minted. Now all units seem to have them for their troops to carry. I think that the Agnes commemorative coin was the first. I challenge anyone to come up with a unit coin that predates Agnes. I have the lead proof of the coin framed on my wall.

On a totally different note, one of my memories of Arnold involved our cats. When my family and I moved to Arnold, we had three cats, of which one mother and her daughter were pregnant. After a month we had three cats and six kittens. I don't think our new neighbors had expected this when they greeted us the first time. After the kittens were about six weeks old I collected three of them and brought them to work with me. They were very curious and in order to see outside, one got on each shoulder and the third got on top of my hat. I was in uniform. All the way into Baltimore people in passing cars were rubbernecking trying to figure out what this colonel was doing. I got to the federal office building, parked my car and rode up the elevator with the kittens still very comfortable in their locations. I walked into my office and was greeted by the secretaries with "Now what?" I told them that it was their responsibility to find new homes for them. All women are nuts over kittens and within ten minutes all three had been claimed by secretaries down the hall. The next day I did it again with the other three kittens.

In the long run I think that as it turned out I was sort of lucky that General Clark didn't send me to New Orleans. I would have had a lot of explaining to do in later years. As they say, be careful what you ask for—you may get it.

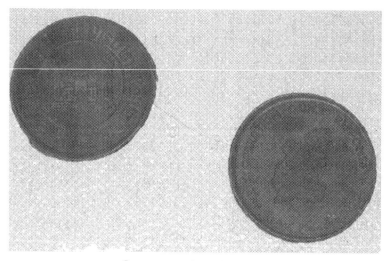

Commemorative coin – 1972

# Chapter 12 – Last tour to
# Germany, 1973 – 1978

I went to Germany as a colonel and returned to the States as a major general. The last few months in the Baltimore district I was selected to attend the Advanced Management Program for Executives at the University of Pittsburgh. This is a unique program at the business school that brings about twenty middle managers from industry and government together for an intensive course in the latest management techniques. Being selected by the army for this course was an indicator that it anticipated my being selected for more responsible positions. Following this course I was shipped to Germany to command the $7^{th}$ Engineer Brigade in Stuttgart. The brigade was part of the army's $7^{th}$ Corps.

The army was undergoing a very stressful period in that it was moving to an all-volunteer force while still having many drafted members. In addition, it was changing all the rules. There was no longer *reveille* or passes. The troops got up when they wanted as long as they showed up for their first duty of the day. At the end of the day they were allowed to leave until the next morning duty. Barracks were out and in their stead were one and two man rooms. It was referred to as a "college campus." Beer and liquor were allowed in the rooms. Beer dispensing machines were even installed in the buildings. The big problem was that the tools that the NCOs had historically used to control the troops were eliminated. No longer could the first sergeant tell a trooper who had screwed up that his pass had been pulled for a week. As a result, the NCOs sat back and said "tell us what you want us to do and we will do it." Unfortunately, the officers didn't have the answers. Couple all of this with a mix of lifers and draftees who didn't mix; it caused us to almost lose the army.

A new soldier would arrive in his unit and be questioned by his peers as to whether he used drugs or alcohol. He was thus grouped accordingly. He was never given the opportunity to select neither. The draftees wanted out of the army as quickly as possible. I had one soldier sent to me by his battalion commander for counseling. He was a smart lad, a college graduate, and obviously very capable. His problem was that he was very insubordinate and was on a course of getting into real trouble. I talked with him and told him that if he continued his ways he could well end up with a courts-martial and a felony conviction. His response was "Will it get me out of the army?"

We had anarchy in the units. There were race riots somewhere nearly every week. One of my battalions was scheduled to move to a training area for a month. The morning they were to move all of the truck tires had been slashed. A lieutenant complained to his company commander that he had been hit in the head by a beer bottle while walking in the company street the previous night. The company commander asked him why he was in the company street at night. It took a couple of years for the army's ship to right itself and get the all-volunteer force to work. In Stuttgart there was a substantial engineer community. Besides the brigade there was an engineer company, the corps' engineer staff and an area engineer office responsible for the maintenance and renovation of facilities. Major Jim Martin was the area engineer. The engineer community formed its own social gatherings with bridge groups and bowling teams. Jim and his wife Shirley were in the same bridge group and bowling team as Peg and me. Some fifteen years later Shirley and I were married. Jim had come down with lung cancer and died in 1981.

I commanded the 7th Engineer Brigade for a little over a year when I was selected for promotion to Brigadier General. This meant that I would be assigned to a general officer position somewhere in the world. Since I had only served but one year of my Germany tour, the powers to be decided to keep me in Germany. The only BG engineer position in Germany was the Division Engineer of the European Division (EUD) of the Corps of Engineers. This was an operating division unlike other corps divisions, which are strictly management divisions. Other corps divisions had several districts under their command. These districts did the work being broadly supported and supervised by their parent division. EUD was like a super district with the responsibility for the military construction for the army and air force in Europe. Projects ranged from Turkey, Greece, Italy, and throughout Germany. This was my assignment in Frankfurt for the next year.

General Blanchard had been the 7th Corps Commander when I commanded the 7th Engineer Brigade. After I had left the 7th Corps, General Blanchard was promoted to four stars and assigned to Heidelberg as the Commander in Chief U.S. Army Europe (CINC USAEUR). MG Dick Groves, the son of LTG Leslie Groves of the Manhattan Project, was the Deputy Chief of Staff, Engineer (DCSENG) for USAEUR. General Blanchard liked engineers and pulled General Groves up as his chief of staff and at the same time selected me to replace General Groves as the DCSENG. So, after only a year at Frankfurt we moved to Heidelberg.

When WWII was over, my father had moved from Paris to Frankfurt. He did not immediately return to the States but remained in Germany until 1947. Mother joined him, and it was in her words like an extended honeymoon. The position he held as a colonel was the same one that I now held in Heidelberg as the engineer for Europe. I visited the commander of the Post Exchange system in Europe and was talking with his secretary. She was questioning me about my name in that she had worked for a colonel after the war that had the same name. When I told her that I was his son she got up from her chair and gave me a big hug.

In 1977 things seemed to thaw a bit with the USSR. General Blanchard invited his counterpart, the Soviet CINC of armed forces in East Germany, to visit West Germany. He arrived in Heidelberg with his full staff. We paired off with our counterparts for a one-week visit. My counterpart was a major general. Each of us had our own interpreter and the conversations were rather light. The Soviets were very suspicious that we were trying to get some intelligence information from them. At dinner one night I asked my counterpart what each of his ribbons stood for. His response was "That was a long time ago." I asked if he had been out of the Soviet Union and was surprised when he said that he had been in Cuba. I started speaking to him in Spanish and his interpreter had a fit. He cut off the conversation. Obviously the interpreter was in control of this major general.

We took the group to a PX in Grafenwoehr where they were allowed to wander around and buy anything they wanted. I looked over to the magazine section and saw them all hunched over a copy of Playboy. There was tremendous interest with lots of grins and laughs. I guess there was no similar publication in the Soviet Union. Grafenwoehr is a training area, and a tank and artillery demonstration was conducted for them. They were particularly impressed with the gun crews and the fact that there were no officers in the crews, only a NCO in charge. Their CINC was offered the opportunity to drive one of our tanks. He accepted, climbed in, and without any instructions spun the tank down the trail, made a U-turn and charged back to the demo area at high speed. He braked it, climbed out, and thanked General Blanchard for the opportunity to drive an American tank. It was obvious that he had had experience with one before. We had lunch in a brigade dining facility where the Soviets were allowed to mix and to talk with anyone they wanted. The Soviet CINC came up to a trooper and asked if he had enlisted or had been drafted. He responded that he had enlisted. He was then asked why he had enlisted and the trooper responded "To serve my country." None of these soldiers had been prompted. In fact, they didn't even know we were coming or who we were. The general brushed a tear away and said, "I haven't heard those words since the Great War."

I met many Nazis during this tour. All officers in the armed forces were Nazis. They took an oath when they were commissioned. One of my best German friends, Franz, was a lieutenant on a U-boat. His father was a professor at the University of Heidelberg, and when Franz informed him of his enlistment in the navy, his father disowned him. It wasn't until several years after the war that he and his father were reconciled. Franz's sub was stationed in the Gulf of Mexico, just off the Mississippi coast. He told of their surfacing at night and sinking whatever was sighted. Then at daylight they would dive to the bottom of the gulf and lie there quietly. One day the surface was particularly calm and his sub was spotted and attacked. It was blown up. Franz and several of the crew escaped using a portable breathing apparatus. Franz was interned at Fort Knox where he spent the remainder of the war. When he returned to Germany he met and married Lisa. Franz told me that one had to be young or crazy to be in the U-boats. Also, he referred to the Nazis as *gangsters*. Lisa and her sister Else had been members of the Hitler Youth. Else told me that all children were expected to join. From what I could tell there was little choice for these kids. I bought a used car for Jacque from a German in Frankfurt. While we were negotiating in his living room he asked me what I thought of the German Waffen SS units. I said that we considered them to have been highly trained and effective units. I avoided the political implications. He said that he had been a member of such and such unit and that he couldn't stand Jews. We bought the car and left.

General Blanchard selected LTG Ken Cooper to be his deputy, another engineer. A year later I was promoted to major general giving the USAEUR staff three senior engineer generals, one lieutenant general, and two major generals. At my promotion ceremony—as General Cooper was pinning on my second star—I commented, "My only regret was that my father was not alive to see this." General Cooper said, "He knows." What a great response.

With LTG Blanchard, 7th Corps Commander
Stuttgart, Germany – 1974

Official photo, Fort Leonard Wood – 1981

Comments

# Chapter 13 – Odds and Ends

## Palm Reader

After I graduated from high school I made good friends with three guys my own age. I had been a life guard at the Chevy Chase Country Club just outside of Washington in Maryland. Don Mackey, Sterling Glenn, and Skip Best were sons of members and spent most of the summer at the pool. We sort of formed a club in that we all dated girls from the club, went to the movies together, and drank beer in Washington. At that time the age limit for beer and wine in Washington was eighteen. When I got an appointment to West Point they rejoiced with me. The night before I was to leave for West Point by train they wanted to take me out to dinner at a fancy downtown restaurant. We arrived and were seated like very special people. The restaurant had been told what this special occasion was and made sure that it indeed was special. They sent around a photographer for individual and group pictures. They each cost about $5, which were big bucks in 1946. After dinner a palm reader came to our table to read each of our hands. She would take each hand one at a time and then look at the wrinkles and creases as she would fold it up. We all found out soon we were to be married, how many children we were going to have, and in general about how long our "life line" was. When she came to me she looked pretty hard and said, "You have a short life line. You will live for another fourteen years." What an awful thing to do to a kid. I calculated that when I was thirty-two I was cashing it in. It wasn't until I was thirty-three that I quit thinking of her. She blew it with me.

# Lobster Newburg

In June of 1947 I had finished Plebe Year at West Point and was about as happy as one could be. I was also very proud of myself for accomplishing a goal that at times I didn't think was possible.

One of the most striking of all the uniforms that we were issued was the *all-whites*. This was white trousers and a high collared blouse. Six sets of trousers were issued when we entered that were worn with the *dress gray* and *full dress gray* blouses but the white blouse was issued only to upperclassmen. After we passed from 4th Classmen to 3rd Classmen we were issued six sets of the white blouses. The whites were cotton and very heavily starched. To open the trouser legs and blouse sleeves we had to use the chrome-plated bayonet that we placed on the end of our rifles when we paraded. We would slide the bayonet up to one edge and slowly work it across to the other until finally it was opened enough to get into. Once in uniform you didn't sit down because that would put creases in it.

When I arrived at West Point in July of 1946, I had one set of clothes and my toilet articles.

After a year of exercise and sports my shape changed dramatically. I could no longer fit into my old civvies, so I went on my first leave carrying only khaki uniforms and one set of dress whites. I even carried the chrome bayonet along.

By coincidence my parents were returning from Germany at the same time my summer leave started. I took the train to Washington and we all stayed at my Aunt Margaret's home. It was a wonderful reunion.

My mother's Uncle Ernest was retired from the Bureau of Standards in Washington, and he lived in the Cosmos Club, a very exclusive club for scientists. The club was also located in a very exclusive part of Washington, opposite the northwest corner of Lafayette Square across from the White House. Uncle Ernest invited the three of us for Sunday dinner at the Cosmos Club. This was the special event at which I would wear my dress whites for the first time. I got out the bayonet, opened up the legs and sleeves, and got out my Blitz cloth to make sure the brass was without a blemish. We drove down to the Cosmos Club, and I made a grand entrance into the dining room. I knew that all eyes were on me. This was my moment of glory.

We were seated at a prominent table, and after a glass of wine we ordered from the menu. I selected Lobster Newburg, one of my all-time favorites. We were promptly served and my plate was large with three points of toast. I took my fork, cut off a corner of the toast, and the entire plate flipped over on my lap. The toast was close to the edge of the plate and my bearing down on it caused it to flip. There I was in the middle of the dining room in dress whites with Lobster Newburg running down my legs onto the carpet. I lifted my plate back to the table and scooped my dinner back to the plate with my hands. The waiter came over and assisted me with several clean towels. When most of it was cleaned up I used my knife to scrape off the remainder. This I had been taught at West Point when something was spilled on one's clothes. When an upperclassman spotted some food that had fallen on a plebe's uniform he would command "PD Dumb Squat" and the plebe would grab his knife and clean off his uniform. PD stood for *police detail*. Here in the middle of Washington I had reverted back to being a plebe.

The worst part was to come. After dinner I had to walk through the dining room and then one block to the car. Lobster Newburg and white ducks don't mix.

Very proud in my highly starched dress whites – June, 1947.

## Little things sometimes have the most impact on your life.

It was January 1950 while eating dinner in Washington Hall, USMA, that there was an announcement from the poop deck: "All first classmen who desire to be commissioned in the air force are required to take the AF physical examination on Thursday morning at the station hospital." This was prior to the establishment of the AF Academy and 25 percent of USMA graduating classes were commissioned in the AF. I showed up early at the hospital and went through the entire procedure of needles, bottles, X-rays, arm cuff, cold stethoscope, coughs, and other indignities. I was in good shape, 20/20 eyes, and passed easily. This was my first step to being an AF Officer.

Two months later on a Saturday morning, I wandered over to the cadet store and saw a set of *pinks and greens* on the plain type pipe racks, size 39 regular with size 30/29 trousers. I was a perfect 39 regular 30/29. I could pick any suit of this size, put it on, and walk away without alterations. I promptly gathered it up, signed the slip debiting my account, and brought them back to the barracks trunk room in the basement of Cadet Division 33. About once a week I would visit my new uniform and visualize a pair of silver wings over the left breast pocket.

One month later, again at dinner at Washington Hall, there came another announcement from the poop deck: "All First Classmen who are to be commissioned in the AF are required to purchase the new AF dress blue uniform." I was stunned because I had in the trunk room a set of pinks and greens that only army officers could wear. Even more distressing was the fact that I had spent my budgeted uniform amount on the wrong uniform. My only solution was to be commissioned in the army. Thus, because I had purchased the wrong uniform, I spent thirty-one years in the army rather than the air force.

# Decisions

After my stint at the Engineer School teaching float bridges I was assigned to the Norfolk District, Corps of Engineers. The idea at the time was to send junior officers to a district for a one-year orientation tour so they would get a taste of big construction and the administration of construction contracts. My duty station was at the district's area office at Langley Air Force Base, Virginia. I was responsible for the management of several minor contracts.

I was promoted to captain, and the district engineer, Colonel Robert B. Warren, called me on the phone and said that he wanted me to move from Hampton to Norfolk and to be the executive officer for the district. The previous exec, a lieutenant colonel, had just retired and he had no other replacement.

The responsibilities of the exec were to manage the office in the absence of the district engineer and to be the contracting officer for all contracts under a certain amount. My orientation in district operations was in high gear.

One day, the North Atlantic Division Engineer, BG Benjamin B. Tally, flew in to Norfolk to check on the progress of the construction of Nike sites being constructed by the district. Those in the Hampton Rhoads area were part of the nationwide program to protect major cities. General Tally and Colonel Warren left the district office for an all-day inspection trip, to return at five.

About 9:30 in the morning it started to snow. About 10:00 it started to snow harder. At 11:00 there was about four inches on the ground. At noon, my administrative assistant came into my office and said, "Captain, it's snowing pretty hard out there." I said, "It sure is." He said "What do you plan to do about it?" I said, "I don't think there is much I can do." He said, "I mean what do you intend to do about the office?" I said, "What do you think I should do about the office?" He said, "We here in Norfolk very seldom see snow like this. The folks down here have no idea how to drive in these conditions. The last time we had such a snow the streets were clogged for hours and some of our folks didn't get home until midnight." I asked what he recommended. He replied, "Close the office and let our employees leave before the rush hour." I said, "You mean let them take annual leave if they wish?" He said, "No, if you close the office then all will be required to leave. None of the time will be charged as personal leave." I asked what it would cost the government in lost time. The answer was about $25,000. I told him to come back in an hour and I would give him an answer.

At 1:00 p.m. he returned for my decision. Snow was starting to pile up. I told him to close the office. In fifteen minutes the parking lot was empty except for my car. At 1:30 the snowing stopped. At 2:00 the bright sun came out. By 4:00 all snow had melted off the street. At 4:45 Colonel Warren arrived back in the office and asked were everyone was. I announced that I had closed the office at one o'clock. He said, "You did what?" I told him that it had been snowing and I thought it was best to let everyone go home early. He said "We will talk about this in the morning" and left. I had a full night to think about my actions.

The next morning I arrived in the office at 7. Colonel Warren arrived at 7:30 and said, "Let's go get a cup of coffee and talk about yesterday." He asked what happened and I gave the story. He asked if I knew what the implications were, and I said that it cost the government about $25,000 in lost wages. Then Colonel Warren did something I have never forgotten. He said "Congratulations. Making decisions is one of the most difficult things you will ever be called upon to do. It is very difficult to find people who will make decisions. I will never criticize you for making a decision. Some of them will turn out bad. When that happens, I will go over with you the information you had in making your decision to see if you used all of the information available to you. But, I was not in your shoes. You were the one responsible for the decision."

Colonel Warren was highly decorated for WWII service in First Infantry Division. I could visualize how he earned his awards. I am sure that he never realized the impact he had on me. I used his philosophy of decision making for the remainder of my career. This was one of the first things that I told my subordinates when I took over a new assignment.

# Hero

Flood Agnes caused a great deal of personal loss. There were thousands of homeless people in many states. Bob Hope came to Baltimore to host a fundraising telethon. This was a twelve-hour nonstop effort on his part and it was a magnificent success. I met Bob at the auditorium where the show was to take place and presented him with a red *Corps of Engineers Emergency Operations* jacket. Our picture appeared in the following week's edition of the *Army Times*.

The event attracted a rather large number of folks who wanted to participate in the activities and to see and possibly meet *the* Bob Hope. I was standing in uniform in the rear of the auditorium when I felt a tug on my trouser leg. I looked down and saw a little boy, no older than three years old, looking at me. He asked, "Are you a hero?" Now, how do you answer a question like that? Even real heroes will deny that they were heroes. They all say that "They were just doing what was expected of them" and something like "The real heroes are the ones that didn't come back." I stumbled around with an answer as his mother looked on with a stern face that said "Don't play games with my kid." I told him that I had received some medals while in combat and that the ribbons on my uniform represented those medals. He looked me over rather closely and then pointed and said, "You mean the ones with the bugs on them?" These were oak leaf clusters for multiple awards. His mother's face turned neutral. I said "Yep, they are the ones." I guess she was satisfied with the answer, the kid was happy in that he had seen a *hero*, and I was happy to get away from it all.

# Anniversary Hike

This is a strange story that happened on our eighteenth wedding anniversary, September 14ᵗʰ, 2006. Eighteen years before, September 14, 1988, Shirley and I were married in St. Louis. We have celebrated each anniversary in different ways: a trip to New Orleans, a trip to Hawaii, and sometimes fishing on the Gasconade River. This year we decided to take a day hike from Steamboat Springs into the Wilderness Area of the Flattop Mountains here in Colorado. I bought Shirley Jean a great backpack that is designed for a special picnic, two each plates, knives, forks, spoons, wine glasses, napkins, a corkscrew, a table cloth, a cheese board and an insulated wine bottle section.

We loaded the backpack with cheese, fruit, a couple of chicken sandwiches, and a special bottle of red wine. At nine o'clock we left in our SUV for the Flattops. I had my backpack loaded with survival stuff, compass, water bottles, first aid kit, rope, duct tape, whistle, and other stuff you need if something unexpected comes up (bears, mountain lions, or getting lost). Shirley Jean had the goody backpack.

We drove about forty miles, twenty of which were on a dirt road, to the trailhead. The weather was a bit threatening with some rain, a bit cool and lots of clouds. As we signed in at the trailhead we weren't too sure that this was a really good way to celebrate our anniversary, but we struck out on our four-mile 1,500-foot vertical rise hike.

After an hour and a quarter we reached our destination, Mosquito Lake, a beautiful mountain lake surrounded by tall aspen trees in full fall yellow color. No sign of even one mosquito. Off the trail we found a nice flat rock big enough for the two of us and the tablecloth with our lunch. The sun came out and the wind stopped. This was just what we were looking for. We opened the red wine, poured two full glasses, and toasted each other for eighteen wonderful years. Just then a sudden gust of wind came up lifting my hat off my head and blowing it about fifteen feet away. I ran over to retrieve it and found that there was a penny underneath it. The penny was rather corroded and covered with dirt. I brought it back, gave it to Shirley, and said, "Look at the date on this penny I just found." It was a 1988 penny. How did this happen that we would find a spot in the wilderness area of the Flattop Mountains, well off the trail, 10,600 feet high where the wind would blow my hat on top of a penny whose date was our wedding year on our eighteenth anniversary? There are some things that only faith can explain. Shirley knows that it was her mother who was with us on the hike and placed the coin under my hat.

Shirley & Me – 2002

# Chapter 14 - My Brother

"Eddie died this morning." Early on the morning of January 6, 1944, Aunt Margaret came into the bedroom and told me that my brother had died, that I didn't have to go to school that morning, and that my parents would soon be there to take Catharine and me back home.

Eddie, Mother's first born, was five years older than me. He had contracted polio when he was three and as a result had a weakened right arm. This didn't seem to bother him much for he developed good strength in his left arm for sports even though he was right-handed. What did bother him was that with his weakened arm he was unable to pass the West Point physical examination. He wanted to be "just like Pop, an army officer." So in 1940, Eddie applied to and was accepted to the military college of South Carolina, the Citadel. Here he hoped to be commissioned through the ROTC program.

We were living in Reno, Nevada, at the time and Charleston, South Carolina was a long way off. There was no way that he would be able to get home for the Christmas holidays, so he spent his Christmas leave in Washington D.C. with my father's sister, Aunt Margaret McKelway, and her family. In the spring of 1941 my father received orders to Fort Belvoir, Virginia; national mobilization was starting up, and Fort Belvoir would be the major training area for engineer troops. Pop was a trainer and a good one. This move brought us back to the D.C. area, close contact with the McKelways, and a place where Eddie would spend the summer with his family.

That summer, Eddie started running a constant temperature and didn't feel well. After several tests, the doctors told Mother that he had tuberculosis. Mother was devastated and hysterical. They also said that he should be sent to Fitzsimmons Hospital in Denver where they treated TB patients. It seems that high elevation environments were the best for healing TB. So in 1941 Eddie was sent to Denver to get well. We would get regular reports of his progress, but one seemed of particular concern: the glands in his neck were swollen. The doctors did a biopsy but I never heard the results. In talking to my mother years later she told me that Eddie had actually had Hodgkin's disease and not TB.

In 1943 the doctors at Fitzsimmons sent Eddie home to Virginia as "cured." I counted the days until his return like I counted days to Christmas. There is a bond between brothers that is difficult to explain. Although we fought, told on each other, and played tricks to get the other in trouble, we missed being together. I longed to be with him and was delighted that he was coming home cured. Eddie arrived by train and the five of us drove together to our home at Fort Belvoir. The next few days we spent getting to know each other again. I set up a horseshoe pit out back where we would spend hours beating each other. Eddie threw the shoes left-handed. We shared the same bedroom, which allowed us to be able to talk well into the night. I needed lots of advice from an older brother since I was in the sixteen-year-old range.

Later in the year, Eddie started to feel poorly again and was placed in the station hospital at Fort Belvoir. After a few weeks the doctors said that it was best for him to be admitted to Walter Reed General Hospital in Washington, D.C. This is the same hospital where Catharine and I were born. I had had a pain in my right great toe for several months and had been seeing a doctor at Walter Reed, and he recommended that I have an operation to remove a tumor on the tip of the toe. The operation was scheduled over the Christmas holiday so that I wouldn't miss any school. I entered the hospital on the 22nd of December for a ten-day stay. This meant that the Prentiss family had two sons in Walter Reed, in different wards, over Christmas. This was a very difficult time for my mother and father.

Eddie was in the isolation ward and I was in the orthopedic ward. What a shock and revelation it was to me to suddenly be living with a group of wounded soldiers. All of them had lost one or more limbs, some just days earlier. Many tried to make fun of their wounds, kidding each other as to who had the best looking stumps. At night, however, I would hear the groans and sobs flowing down the hallways. The realities of the war had come home to me.

On Christmas day I asked the nurse if I could visit my brother. I told her that he was in another ward. She said that she saw no reason and would make arrangements for me. Later that day she told me that he was in an isolation ward that allowed no visitors. She looked at me rather strangely and never again joked around during my stay in the hospital. She knew what was to come.

On the day that I left the hospital my father picked me up and said, "Let's go see Eddie." I told him that I had tried to see him but wasn't allowed because he was in an isolation ward. He said that was no problem and we went hand in hand into Eddie's room. I was absolutely shocked. Eddie was in an oxygen tent trying to eat some Jell-O. His hand was shaking so that the Jell-O would fall off the spoon. He did recognize me, and we chatted for a few minutes and left. On the way home my father said that he looked happier that day than he had seen him in several weeks. That was the last time I saw Eddie. When we got back to Fort Belvoir I told Catharine of my visit with Eddie. I don't think that she realized how grave the situation was. All she said was "Oh."

Eddie loved music, particularly classical music. During his last days he said he could hear beautiful music. He had never heard the songs but was so taken by the beauty that he asked my mother to put her ear next to his so she could hear it also.

On the 4$^{th}$ of January my father told us that we were going to stay with the McKelways for a few days and that he and my mother were to stay at the guest house at Walter Reed. Catharine and I moved in with Aunt Margaret. I prayed for my brother's health all the next day and night. I heard the early phone call on the morning of the 6$^{th}$ but only heard Aunt Margaret's muffled voice. When she came in my room I knew what she was going to say. Catharine and I got up, had breakfast and went to the basement and played ping-pong together not saying a word. Later my mother and father arrived to pick us up. Mother was completely overcome with grief, saying over and over to me that I was the man in the family now.

We piled into the car, drove to a funeral home where my father made the arrangements, and drove home to Fort Belvoir. We went into the house and we all went to our bedrooms. I could hear Catharine crying and my mother sobbing. I did my own into my pillow. I picked up Eddie's shaver and found tiny pieces of his beard left from its last use. Since my father decided that Eddie would be cremated that day, this was all that remained of Eddie. I blew the shaver clean and put my head in the pillow again.

The funeral was two days later at the little chapel at the Arlington National Cemetery. A soldier in dress blues carried the urn with Eddie's ashes out of the chapel. My father leaned over to me and said "Eddie would have called him a jerk."

Mother never got over Eddie's death. My father left a couple of months later to the war in Europe. Every night while studying in my room I could hear the sobs coming from downstairs as Mother would write to her husband across the sea fighting a war. Mother's rationalization of Eddie's death was that he was a casualty of war. With sons dying each day in the war, somehow Mother felt that Eddie played his part too and that made it right.

Eddie at CMTC camp – San Luis Obispo, 1940

Eddie at CMTC camp – San Luis Obispo, 1940

Eddie – Reno, 1940

Comments

# Chapter 15 – My Father and Mother

I originally intended to write about my father and mother separately but the more I thought about it, I felt that it would be too difficult to separate them. Their lives were so entwined that there would be a point and counterpoint.

Pop was a fourth generation Washingtonian born in Washington. Actually he was a sixth generation Washingtonian, but the first two were born in Boston before George created Washington, D.C. When the nation's capital was first established there was no housing for all of the new federal employees, so George Washington asked William Prentice and Joseph Greenleaf, two bankers in Boston, to come to Washington to build housing. They came and built the first row houses in the capital. In the early 1950s much of the housing they built was torn down with the urban renewal of SW Washington. One row, The Wheat Row, was retained and is on the National Record of Historic Places. It was named the Wheat Row because the end house was named for its owner, a sea captain named Wheat. William Prentiss married Eunice, the daughter of his partner, and this started the chain of Prentiss's in Washington. The name changed with their son William Jr. to Prentiss. He had Charles Prentiss, who had William Prentiss, who had Louis W. Prentiss, who had Louis W. Prentiss, Jr. That would be me.

Mother was a Maryland Bowie. The Bowie farm is what is now Fort Meade and Bowie, Maryland. Through the Bowie line I have been able to trace the family to Priscilla Mullins and John Alden of the Mayflower saga and thence to the ninth century Normans. The famous Jim Bowie was a brother in our clan, but when he was killed at the Alamo, he left no family survivors because his wife and children had died of cholera.

Pop met Mother's sister Margaret (Pop also had a sister, Margaret) on a tennis court. He asked her if he could visit that evening at her home. She agreed and he arrived after dinner. Mother was there, and Pop took a fancy to her over her sister, so the next dates were with Mother. Pop was going to Colorado School of Mines and Mother was going to the University of Wisconsin. Mother had other boyfriends including one who was quite rich. He had a Stutz Bearcat Roadster convertible in which Mother said that they rode all around Washington strutting their stuff. She really was in love with Pop, though, and they were married on the 28th of December, 1921, after Pop had been commissioned a 2nd lieutenant.

Their first home was at Fort Knox, Kentucky. It was a WWI company mess hall with a coal-fired stove used for both heating and cooking. Pop obtained some plywood and put up walls so as to have a bedroom and a living room. Mother mentioned to me several times that it was so difficult to have clean clothes. She would wash them by hand and then hang them out to dry on the clothesline. When she brought them in they were black with coal dust. All of Fort Knox was heated with soft coal.

Catharine and Eddie were both born in Washington. Soon after Catharine's birth, Pop was assigned to the Canal Zone. The next year Mother took her two children to visit to her parents in Berkeley, California. Mother's sister Sue, only a year older than Eddie, became ill while Mother was visiting. She was later diagnosed as having polio. When Mother returned to the Zone, both Eddie and Catharine also came down with polio. Eddie ended up with a weakened right arm but Catharine was not affected. Years later when I would visit Mother I got the feeling that she felt guilty about the trip to Berkeley. "If I hadn't gone there, they wouldn't have gotten polio."

Pop and Mother loved their family and loved each other deeply. I have letters that Pop wrote when he was attending the Signal School at Fort Monmouth, New Jersey. Mother was pregnant with Eddie and stayed in Washington with her parents. These are classic love letters and are quite touching. They were in Mother's 1922 diary, folded and placed according to the date written. I'm sure that it never occurred to Pop that his youngest son would be reading them eighty-four years later. I also have the diaries that they wrote in the early thirties. Part of army tradition is not to display affection in public. At West Point the penalty for being seen holding hands with your drag (date) was five demerits. Around home was different. Pop would pull Mother over to sit on his lap and smooch—much to the disgust of their three children. Pop always kissed Mother Good-bye in the morning and hello in the evening.

Reading these vignettes, you cannot help but notice that I referred to my father as *Pop* and to my mother as *Mother*. The role of family Disciplinarian fell to Mother. Pop was brought in when there was a serious infraction or when Mother would say, "Go talk to your son." When Pop was brought in, it was straight talk with no misunderstandings as to what he meant. Thus, Pop got the more endearing name and Mother got the proper name for her position. Pop never struck us, but Mother used the back of her hair brush on our tails. She also had a little leather pony whip with which she would switch our bare legs. During one of my last visits to her before she died we were reminiscing, and she said that we would go around telling everyone, "Our mother horse whips us." The pony whip was lost from the car during our trip from Golden to San Francisco. Arley, the maid, went with us and Mother figured Arlie threw it out the car window. I think Eddie did it.

Pop was very musically talented. He played a ragtime piano by ear, could double whistle just about any song, and at one time he played the guitar. If a party started to slow down, Pop would get on a piano and rev it up, getting folks into a sing-along. In the mid fifties, Pop came home one evening, parked his car in the garage, went outside, and pulled the overhead door down. Just before the door closed, he reached up with his left hand to keep the door from slamming down. He caught the tip of his middle finger in the crack between two panels. The doctors removed the first joint at Walter Reed. This affected his piano playing but he soon adapted to it and was able to continue playing. A few years later he was clearing snow from the driveway with a snow blower. It was a wet snow and the discharge became clogged. Not thinking, Pop reached in to unclog it and cut the ends off three fingers on his right hand. This ended Pop's piano playing. Mother, of course, was upset and on the way to the hospital to visit him she said, "He just keeps chipping away."

Mother was also smart and had a very quick mind. In the mid thirties, Mother read a book on nutrition and that changed her life, and ours, forever. She bought a large pressure cooker that she used every day. Most foods were cooked quickly to preserve their vitamins. Every morning we got a tablespoon of wheat germ in our milk. On the right side of our plate there would be a cod liver oil capsule, a vitamin B-complex tablet, and a Di-calcium-phosphate tablet. Also there was a glass of fresh orange juice. She would periodically check the palm of our hands to see if we were getting enough carotene in our diet. If you did, then your palms would have a yellow hue. This was part of our breakfast until we left home for college. It certainly worked for Mother. She was nearly one hundred years old when she died, never had a broken bone, and had all of her teeth. Some parts wore out, however. She had lost most of her eyesight and hearing. She had to give up bowling when she was eighty-four because her knees were giving out.

Mother absolutely hated to be kidded. She felt that those who were kidding were cruel, that this was their way of inflicting their cruelty upon her and she had no defense. She never forgot such events or those who did it to her.

Pop loved to work with his hands. He would attempt most any project, learning as he went along. He would buy old furniture, often in a gunny sack, restore and upholster it. Several of the beautiful antiques in our home now were bought as "firewood." Pop would cane straight-back chairs. It wasn't until several years later that I showed him that he would only need to weave one of the four horizontal and vertical runs. He gave me a look of pride that I was one up on him. I had read it in a book. Pop helped me build a soap box derby car in Reno. I came in second and missed out going to Akron, Ohio, to the nationals by a half a box. Doing things with us was a priority for Pop. He taught us weapons safety and even set up a target range in the basement for use with the Benjamin Pump pellet guns he bought us. We all became quite proficient shots. I have a box of Eddie's stuff with marksmanship medals he won in 1940 at the Citizens Military Training Corps (CMTC) summer camp at San Luis Obispo, California.

Both Mother and Pop were very frugal. They were influenced heavily by the Depression. We were relatively well off because Pop had a salary. There wasn't any money to spare, however. One of my jobs in Golden was go into the yard and pick dandelion greens for a salad. "Only the young ones," Mother would say. I cannot recall ever eating an individual steak until I entered West Point. Steak for Mother was a large sirloin placed on a platter in front of Pop, who would cut it into five pieces. We never had hamburgers; they were *meat cakes* which were more round than flat. We had liver once a week and none of us liked it. One of the rules of the house was that you ate "everything on your plate." The dining room table was a walnut expandable table with leaves. The three of us found small "shelves" under the tabletop where the table had been expanded. Here is where much of the unwanted liver was dispatched. When we moved and the movers hauled the table out to the van out fell little pieces of liver leather. Mother watched us more closely after that.

One evening in Reno Mother had been shopping for the dinner meal. She had decided that we would have a tripe stew. These types of meat were always the least expensive. She would periodically buy liver, beef heart, and beef kidneys. Eddie would complain and ask, "Why do we always have to have innards?" The answer was "Because they are good for you." This was the first time that she had ever brought home tripe. She got out the pressure cooker, sliced up the tripe, cut up potatoes, celery, and carrots and cooked away. As we were seated around the table the aroma of tripe stew floated from the kitchen to the dining room. It wasn't the kind of smell that stimulated the saliva glands or generated an expectation of a fine meal. Mother served us all a bowl and then one for herself. No one said anything and Mother started in eating. She took one bite, put her spoon down on the plate and said, "We don't need to eat this stew. I will make scrambled eggs for everyone." We were all relieved, especially my father. Mother put the stew in a bowl for Duke who gobbled it down and promptly went into the living room and threw up all over the Chinese rug. We never had tripe again.

Any time that salt was spilled, Mother would take a pinch and throw it over her shoulder. She was very superstitious. When there was a new moon she would "show it some silver" over her shoulder for good luck. I never have understood why these things had to be over the shoulder. She always made a wish on the first star and sealed it with the name of an author. I always used Baum, the author of *The Wizard of Oz*. One day a bird got into the house and Mother had a fit. A bird in a house was a very bad omen foretelling death in the household. When Mother would walk the dogs she would constantly look for four-leaf clovers. Now when I go through some of her books I will find four-leaf clovers carefully wrapped in waxed paper and pressed by the book.

I have never heard anyone else use the word *delicious* the way Mother did. Delicious had nothing to do with what something tasted like. It referred to an experience. A view could be delicious. A story would be delicious. She would say, "I had the most delicious time at the beach." Her grandchildren were very special to her. They would take her into their confidence and tell her all their secrets. When they would leave she would call us and say, "I had such a delicious time with your children."

Mother had a rather strange trait of giving but not quite letting go. If she gave me something there was always a *quid pro quo*. She had to get something back in return. At the end of my last year at West Point my parents bought me a new 1950 Ford as a graduation present. After I had received delivery and wrote to them about how beautiful it was and how much I appreciated it, Mother wrote back saying that now I had to quit smoking. All through her life she would say things like "I will do this for you but only if you do this for me."

Pop had a wonderful sense of humor. He always was able to find something funny in just about any situation even when it was serious or sad. Pop's comment about the soldier carrying Eddie's urn is an example. People liked to be around him because he was fun. He liked all sorts of humor, puns, jokes and stories. One time when I was in the second grade I came home and talked about a new friend, Rein Ladwig. Pop said he must be "orange juice without the orange." Now this was a bit deep for a second grader, so he had to explain that "orange juice without the orange was juice." I still didn't get it so he further explained that he was saying *Jewish*. I asked "What is Jewish?" and he dropped the subject. He had gotten in too deep and wasn't prepared to go into a discussion of the religions of the world. He did not kid because he felt, like Mother, that this was not humor but cruelty. He was spontaneous, sometimes a bit off color, or slightly racial in his humor. Never was he harsh or crude in his stories or jokes. One of his friends and colleagues told me of an occasion when they entered a restroom together and went into separate stalls. Evidently Pop rather exploded and his friend in the next stall called over and said, "You really had a boomer there." Pop's reply was "Too bad I didn't have my pants down."

Mother was a clipper. She loved to read and anytime she found something interesting in a newspaper or magazine she would clip it out. The clippings would be placed in all sorts of odd places—boxes, books and jars. There didn't seem to be any organization as to where these clippings were filed. I pulled out Pop's Masonic Bible and out fell a clipping from the *Washington Evening Star*. Aunt Margaret's husband, Uncle Ben, was the managing editor of the *Star* and his youngest son, John, was a writer who wrote "The Rambler." This was a great job for John because he could pick what he wanted as a subject. His column came out on Wednesdays and Fridays. The clipping that fell out of the Bible was written in the early '60s and told about John and me skinny-dipping in Rock Creek Park in 1942. It seems that Theodore Roosevelt had done the same thing while walking with the French Ambassador. As I leaf through little stacks of yellowed newspaper I find an article about "The White House Green Room," "Delaware's Jewel on the Bay," "Publisher John Hay Whitney's Stylishly Formal Manhattan Town House" and yet another on "Whales, Whaling and Whaleships." Her interests were very broad.

Pop had a little saying that he would use at the appropriate moment. When he was growing up he had a gramophone and he had records of stories that he would play. One was about a very heavy woman who lived in Philadelphia. The story went that it was a very hot day in Philadelphia and the woman was sleeping upstairs in her house. The end of the story was: "the perspiration from her body drowned her three little children in the parlor below. Oh my, what a warm day." So, any time it was an exceptionally warm day Pop would say "Oh my, what a warm day." Also, he used an expression from another story. He never told us what the story was about but it ended with "Jesus Christ Miss Agnes." He would use this expression whenever there was a frustrating situation around the house. This was about as close as he ever came to swearing. When I was stationed at Fort Belvoir in the late '50s, we got a basset hound that I named Miss Agnes. When we moved to Fort Leavenworth, Miss Agnes was adopted by Mother and Pop. I don't think he ever used the Miss Agnes expression after that.

Pop – 1919

Mother – 1919

Mother at Fort Humphries – 1930

Pop and Mother over the center jump.
Mother won 1st in Ladies Jumping on Bermuda – 1930 Comments

# Chapter 16 – My Sister

## Catharine Prentiss Plummer

Ever since my grandfather, my mother's father, died I have had this feeling that as long as someone thinks of that person they haven't really died. There is some part of them that suddenly springs to life from that line that they walked across. Thus, I frequently think of my grandparents, parents, brother, and now my sister, Catharine. As I sit here at the computer she is sitting just in back of me with a smile saying "Happy, what are you up to now?" In our family we never called her anything but Catharine and I was always called Happy or Hap. After we left the family for college and marriage we adopted new identities of Katy and Lou.

I know of Catharine's early life only from my mother. Catharine was Mother's second born arriving in 1924. My arrival was in 1927. Mother reflected that she was a rather frail baby and neighbors had grave concerns as to her survival. However, after a few months Catharine blossomed into a beautiful and healthy little girl. Catharine was born at Walter Reed Army Hospital, as were Mother's other two. Pop was stationed at Fort Meyer, VA just across the Potomac River from Washington D.C. In 1924, Pop was ordered to The Canal Zone, Panama. Mother took Eddie and Catharine for a visit to her parents in Berkeley, California. Susan, mother's youngest sister, contacted a mild case of polio, which was passed on to both Eddie and Catharine. When mother and the kids returned to Panama, both Eddie and Catharine showed signs of the disease and were hospitalized.

Catharine was very lucky in that she recovered without any effects of the paralyzing disease.

The family returned to the States in 1927 and again Pop was stationed at Fort Meyer. I was born in December that year. We moved to Fort Humphries, Virginia, where I have my first memories. Eddie, Catharine, and I were close siblings. We did many things together with Eddie always being the leader, Catharine always being the pacifier, and I being the rebel. One of the things I do remember is Mother putting us together in the bath tub. My excitement was such that she never did that again.

We moved to Golden, Colorado, which was a wonderful outdoor world for all of us. Catharine was very clever and handy in doing crafts. She had her own miniature Singer sewing machine, and she actually made a dress for herself, a blue print with buttons down the front. When she wore it I always bragged to our playmates that she had made it. Diaries were very much in vogue in the early '30s and Catharine had hers, always locked with a little key. I would hope that it still exists and he or she in possession of it would transcribe it and add to this writing. I plan to add all of the pictures of her that I have. In Omaha she decided to get into the publishing business. Pop bought her a jelled copying system that took like a mimeograph master that was placed on the jellied sheet. From that one could copy about fifty copies. She called her newspaper "The Saturday Post" and distributed it weekly—free—to each house in the neighborhood. It contained little stories about neighborhood happenings, a sports section, and her editorial about anything she wanted. She requested input for a story with a prize for the best. John McKelway, Pop's sister's son, wrote a long fictional story that ran for several weeks and won the competition. I think he received a dollar. Catharine was also a collector. Her favorite was to send away for samples of most anything. She had little boxes of corn flakes and the like, lip stick, toothpaste, and most anything that was free for a mail-in one-cent post card. She kept her collection for many years, and it may still be with her possessions. Somewhere along the way a mouse got into the corn flakes and nibbled a hole and consumed the flakes.

Catharine was always a good athlete. She was always able to play right along with us boys and was always a top pick when we were choosing up sides. In Reno she took up skiing along with the rest of the family and became quite good. In high school she was a member of the ski team and competed in regular competitions. One time she came home with a gold medal for first place in the giant slalom. This was a cause for great celebration in the family. On further inquiry she revealed that she was the only one entered in that event in her age group. We were all still proud of her. In college, Catharine took up tennis in earnest and became quite good. She continued to play well into her seventies. A *Washington Post* photographer snapped a picture of her returning a hard serve with grace, and it was printed in the Sunday sports section. She got quite a bit of fan mail as a result. One relative wrote her admiring her *gams*. I had never heard the expression and mother explained that it was slang for legs.

The two colleges that she attended were Mary Baldwin and George Washington in the District of Columbia. At GW she majored in physical education, which was a natural for her. After graduating she took a position as a PE instructor at a private girl's school in the Kalarama section of Washington. When Pop returned from the war in Europe he was assigned to Omaha as the district engineer of the Omaha District, Corps of Engineers. Catharine moved to Omaha to be with her parents. It was here in 1949 that a dashing cavalryman, Walt Plummer, swept her off her feet, proposed, and married her. The rest of her story is best told by those of her new family.

# Appendix A: Comments

Chapter 1
**From:** Martie Shea
**Sent:** Sunday, October 1, 2006 7:53 p.m.
**To:** Lou Prentiss
**Subject:** Re: Memories of Golden
I never knew you lived in Colorado!! No, I don't tire from your stories so please, keep them coming! And as you remember more, edit them. I think the story of your rope and fall is priceless. What you three did as youngsters rivals anything your three daughters did!
XOXO
Marti

Chapter 2
**From:** Dean Paquette
**Sent:** Tuesday, October 3, 2006 7:45 p.m.
**To:** lprentiss2@cox.net
**Subject:** Re: Memories of San Francisco
I enjoy your memoir. You certainly had an interesting childhood. I can tell you that had I broke any windows I would still not be able to sit down.

What a beautiful place to live. In 1971 I was the construction guy for R&D, Gen Betts was my boss. You and I had the boat and you were with the vice chief. (That's another story) R&D wanted to build a modern facility at the Presidio and I put it in the budget. Letterman General had been rebuilt the year before. I was a LTC and I was accompanied by the budget officer of R&D.

We had lots of briefings, including the fact we could not build over 3 stories as the City of San Fran would lose a view of the bay and that was prohibited! However, we were asked to see MG Hughes, a doctor and CO of Letterman. He was anxious and frustrated. He told me that one of the caveats of our new construction was removal of his quarters and a couple of other old quarters. He said, "Come with me," we did and went to his beautiful old quarters. He regarded it a sacrilege to demolish the prominent old quarters. I agreed as I knew it would take years to replace the buildings and somebody in OCE was stupid. I told the General I would handle it and his quarters would remain.

I went back to DC and briefed Gen Betts. I told him I had a lot of influence with Bob Sykes, Chairman of the MILCON Committee in the House. I pulled it off and I hope the quarters are still there.

**From:** David Pettit
**Sent:** Friday, October 27, 2006 8:54 p.m.
**To:** Lou Prentiss
**Subject:** Re: Memories of San Francisco
Last night I had dinner with classmates Bob Hughes (his wife Carolyn died recently) and Dick and Carol Stuart. I was in the middle of telling them about your writing your memories and how I could identify with the general mood of your upbringing when our server announced his name was Terry. I told everyone about your friend Terry Bull and that got a big laugh.

Chapter 3
**From:** Lawrence Applebaum
**Sent:** Wednesday, September 27, 2006 2:36 a.m.
**To:** Lou Prentiss
**Subject:** Memories of Omaha
Dear Lou,
Good story. We also taught our daughters to answer the telephone correctly. We also trained them to give their name so people calling would know that they were not speaking to Monika. The standard answer was, Major Applebaum's quarters, Linda speaking.

Your stories bring back many nice memories.

Sincerely, Larry

Chapter 6
**From:** Walter Plummer
**Sent:** Sunday, November 12, 2006 1:37 p.m.
**To:** Lou Prentiss
**Subject:** Memories of Germany: 1950 – 1953

Hap: Those days in Germany are days that neither we nor our successors will ever see again. I go back just a bit further … to August 1949 and the 10 months preceding the invasion of Korea. You may recall something similar in the peacetime Army of the 30s (From Here to Eternity). No alerts! Wednesday p.m. for athletics (golf/softball/whatever) and, at least in the Constabulary, Saturday a.m. for inspection, complete with varnished helmets, pinks and greens bloused into brown leather boots, yellow scarves and gloves, etc., etc. But, with the invasion of S. Korea, it all changed, forever. I remember the series of meetings over the weekend and the Monday a.m. formations at the Ammo Dump where we loaded our vehicles with the complete basic load of ammo. And, we suddenly became conscious of our dependents and of the necessity for their evacuation if "the balloon were to go up." Subsequently, we lived with it so long that it's difficult to recall what it was really like in the "salad days." Walt

**From:** Edward West
**Sent:** Saturday, November 11, 2006 7:49 a.m.
**To:** Lou Prentiss
**Subject:** RE: Memories of Germany

I particularly enjoyed the encounter with Sgt. Konk and your vivid description, Lt.

It reminded me of my first fire fight after joining A Co., 8th Engr. Bn., 1st Cav. Div. in the Naktong Perimeter. We were deployed as Infantry, in a defensive position, and we were attacked. I had taken the platoon over a few hours before the fire fight began. As the enemy came up the hill, I demonstrably fired my 45 to set the example. I fired away till the platoon Sgt (I didn't even know his name at the time), asked "Lt., what the hell are you trying to accomplish with that p shooter?"

We survived the fire fight, and learned something. Getting fire support (mortar, Artillery, air) was not easy for an Engineer platoon, in a remote position. We went into reserve a few days later. By that time I had identified the platoon's most ingenious, personable trader. I sent him out with a truck load of mines to trade for 50 cal. machine guns, Bazookas, and mortars, all, with lots of ammo. We went back on the line a few days later after learning the rudiments of these new weapons. I was cussed out roundly and soundly when it took two extra trips up the hill, for most of us, to get our new arsenal into position. We were attacked early the following morning. We waited until the last moment and then let loose with everything at the same time. It was a slaughter and the enemy hightailed it after the first salvo. I was in command after that and no one ever complained again about an extra trip up the hill.

Keeping resupplied with ammo was a challenge.

Chapter 7
From: David Pettit
Sent: Tuesday, October 03, 2006 5:14 p.m.
To: Lou Prentiss
Subject: Re: Memories of Belvoir
Excellent. Did you send a copy to Bob Hughes? If not, may I show this to him?

You reminded me of 1943 when my mom and I lived in Alexandria. For one summer I had to take the bus to Belvoir once a week to take piano lessons. I certainly remember the walk from the old PX both ways. My teacher was Rosamond Davis. I think they lived in Quarters 5 or 6. Perhaps you remember them. (His name was Hoy). After the lesson, Rosamond and I would play tennis on the court in the main loop across from where you lived. Incidentally, we lived in #7 in the old area in 1934 and moved to #48 when they were completed in 1935. I forget which House you lived in 1956, but it was near our house. I forget what they called that area in 1956. They became "prized" houses. One of my earliest memories is falling down a step into the living room. I remember that many people complained about that step.

I am slightly confused. In 1941 weren't you at the Belvoir School in seventh grade? I was only there from Feb – April. You probably don't remember but Dad went to school at Belvoir then, a short course, and we lived in a wing of a private home near Mount Vernon. 1941 was one of the highlights of my life.

(Once I plotted my life on graph paper. I had many peaks and troughs!) It was December 41 – March 42 that your father and mine were roommates at Leavenworth.

From: Martie Shea
Sent: Tuesday, October 03, 2006 6:52 p.m.
To: Lou Prentiss
Subject: Re: Memories of Belvoir
Hi Dad,

I like the part about your explorations of Ft. Belvoir—the historic

Discoveries of a little boy of the brick passage way—who knows who else has ever seen what you saw … and finding the cannon balls and then donating them for the cause of the war? How awesome.

You are documenting history. That is what I find so fascinating. And you are telling tales that I have never heard before. And I am wanting to hear more. What you may think are so mundane or so unimportant are so important to me and you just don't realize what they may mean to our future generations. And the written word will last forever. Grandmother's spoken word is priceless, but the VCR technology is going by the wayside and our future grand and great-grandchildren may never be able to view her picture or words. Your written word is forever. It is so important. So even if she has already stated it, I think it is important that you reiterate it as well. So keep writing. Keep writing. I want to read more!

You are telling me more about Grandfather and Grandmother than I ever knew. I never knew that either of them rode horses. No wonder Greta and Barb have that gift! And I now know more of the mementos that you have in your possession.

They meant nothing to me until now. Your stories bring them to life. Now you know why I am excited!

Perhaps I may be your only daughter that has this passion, and I may only be the one expressing it; I'm certain Jacque and Barb appreciate what you are doing for our family.

So please, keep your stories coming. Monica has told me that she has never ever read anyone's memoirs before. She is reading them. She may not be responding, but she has earned her gold stars and that tells you that she is studying very, very hard as well. I think that she has a bit of Grandfather's genes. I didn't know that he was #1 in all of his classes until you wrote it down!

Wow, we have an awesome family!

Love,
Marti

**To:** Lou Prentiss
**From:** Earl Dille
**Subject:** RE: Memories of Germany
These are really good. You should put them all together and call the book "My Army Career" or something like that. New shavetails would be sure to buy it at the PX.

Chapter 8
**From:** Dean Paquette
**Sent:** Saturday, December 9, 2006 4:09 p.m.
**To:** lprentiss2@cox.net
**Subject:** Re: Korea
I have enjoyed reading your memoirs. Very interesting. I hope you provide me with a copy of the finished product. I will, of course, pay a reasonable price. I have written a lot but am only up to my command in Korea. Lots more to do.

That brings me to an incident that occurred in Korea. Bob Wilson and I, with help from Dan Raymond built 2 water nonpotable systems in the 7th Division area. After we finished the first one at Casey I took command of A Co up north of the 38th just outside Camp Kaiser. Kaiser had the Third INF Battle Group and an Armored Cav Sqdn. My Company was located just outside of Kaiser. In addition to my other duties I was ordered to build another water system. Wilson and I worked our ass off getting everything to provide a large shower room for the troops.

One of my major problems was a consistent water source. I had geologists up to Kaiser and all of my officers looking for a site. I heard there was a water drilling unit in 8<sup>th</sup> Army so I went to look for it. I used aircraft and vehicles, and finally found one of our Advanced Course classmates (can't remember his name) who had access to the water drilling equipment. He said it was being used to build a golf course! I asked how we could get the equipment long enough to solve our problem. He said General Decker gave the golf course top priority and he would not help me. I was, and still am pissed off. I asked Raymond to hit his contacts but he also failed.

Now, I find out you owned the equipment. What would you have done??

All the best, B6. PS I eventually found a seeping spring and dug a humongous hole. As the hole filled we pumped the water up to the staved tank.

Chapter 9
**From:** David Pettit
**Sent:** Thursday, October 26, 2006 4:56 a.m.
**To:** Lou Prentiss
**Subject:** Re: Memories
If you write about your IAGS tour please send me a copy. When I first got in the Engineers Col Bathurst, a friend of our parents told me I could have any Lt's job in Panama. I really wanted to do mapping, but I was "warned" by everyone that it would be a "dead-ender." Consequently I went into a combat engineer unit as a platoon commander. I have always listed that as one of my three worst decisions. I am not sure how coveted a job it was, but for me it would have been perfect. (And I would have been the head of a country team) Do you remember that my uncle Frank was in command of IAGS just prior to this?

Chapter 10
**From:** Barb Peterson
**Sent:** Sunday, December 10, 2006 9:55 a.m.
**To:** Lou Prentiss
**Subject:** RE: Viet Nam
Thanks Dad, this one was truly the most insightful. I don't recall you're ever talking about Viet Nam so reading about your firsthand experience was very moving. We did see it on the TV every night. Mom would put the news on so she could hear about the day's events. We knew about where

you were located and if that area made the news she'd go upstairs … it only now has dawned on me that perhaps she went upstairs to cry in private … You know that this is the time when her drinking was awful—nearly every night—I think she couldn't deal with what might happen to you. I greatly appreciate your service to our country so we can live in a relatively free society … you know you are my hero. Love, Barb

Chapter 12
**From:** Martie Shea
**Sent:** Saturday, November 11, 2006 2:19 p.m.
**To:** Lou Prentiss
**Subject:** Re: next version of 1973-1978
Wow, Dad, interesting read! I'm printing it off so that Tom can read it, too.

I'm learning so much—I was wondering if you had run out of stories, time, and energy or just taken me off of your list! Thanks again for sharing this one. I like your impressions— your thoughts of the Russians—what they must have been thinking, especially when you began to speak Spanish and were cut off! How telling was that??? I particularly like the ending. Yes, Grandfather knows. And He was smiling, I'm sure. Love,

Marti

Chapter 14
**From:** CBrittingham
**Sent:** Sunday, September 17, 2006 8:51 a.m.
**To:** Lou Prentiss
**Subject:** Grandpa
Grandpa,

Wow, those are two truly amazing stories. I hadn't heard much about Great Uncle Eddie. Although I have been by to visit him and my great grandparents on several occasions. I never received more than a reason to why he died. I had no idea he was such a strong individual who pushed through something that difficult. Simply incredible, I wish I could have met him. And as for the penny, it sounds to me like you were just where God wanted you to be at that exact moment. Well, I am underway again. I love reading stories like those, I mean ones that are family related. So if you have anymore, please share. This underway kind of snuck up on me. I just had so much to do after I got back from that trip to see Mom and Bruce. I owe you a phone call and I will give you a ring when I pull in next. Not too far from now. Well I got to run. I'll talk to you soon.

Love,
Chris

**From:** Barb Peterson
**Sent:** Saturday, September 16, 2006 9:44 a.m.
**To:** Lou Prentiss
**Subject:** RE: My Brother
Dad … this is so moving and poignant. Thank you for writing and sharing it with us.… I'll save and treasure it as part of our family stories.… I love you, Barb

From: Helen Lee
Sent: Friday, September 15, 2006 7:47 p.m.
To: Lou Prentiss
Subject: Re: My Brother
Dear Uncle Lou,

I am so grateful that you would share this beautiful essay about Uncle Eddie. It is very touching. Ever since I've been small and knew that you and my mother had another brother, I've wondered about Uncle Eddie. Grandmother and I were very close, and she would talk to me about Uncle Eddie and would invariably break down and weep. Once I had children of my own, I realized the enormity of Grandmother's loss. I also realized that when we lose our dear ones to untimely death, we never get over it—we may learn to live with the pain, and accommodate the sorrow in our lives, but we don't get over it. Grandmother gave me some of Eddie's things—I have his prayer book and a diary from when he was around ten, and I treasure them. Fred and I were in Charleston two weeks ago and took a tour through the Citadel and I thought of Eddie then. Thank you again for thinking of me and sharing this testimony to his memory.

I love you,
Helen

**From:** Lawrence Applebaum
**Sent:** Wednesday, September 27, 2006 3:51 a.m.
**To:** Lou Prentiss
**Subject:** AW: Memories
Dear Lou,

What a wonderful story about your brother Eddie. The last page of the story brought tears to my eyes. My own brother is five years older than I am.

Sincerely,
Larry

From: Walter Plummer
Sent: Thursday, January 4, 2007 6:56 p.m.
To: Lou Prentiss
Subject: Re: Home
I am very familiar with the CMTC. I attended the camps at Ft. Crook (now Offutt AFB) in 1939 (Basic) and 1940 (White). I had a tremendous advantage over the other attendees because of my Junior ROTC training at North High. If you recall, the four years were called Basic, Red, White, and Blue. I won the award of Best Basic in 1939 and was allowed to skip the Red course and come back in 1940 as a White. I won the award as Best White and so was permitted to skip the Blue course and take the extension course leading to a commission ... that's how I ended up as a 2nd Lt in March 1942! I remember very clearly my Basic year in 1939 ... the Blues that year included several University of Nebraska football players who had been in Senior ROTC at UN. Of course, all of us were avid football fans and it was quite a treat for us to have Johnny Dodd and Herm Rohrig (to name only two) serving as platoon leaders. As Maurice Chevalier Might have said ..."(CMTC), Ah yes, I remember it well."

Chapter 15
From: Carl Baswell
Sent: Thursday, November 9, 2006 7:29 a.m.
**To:** lprentiss2@cox.net
**Subject:** RE: Memories
Lou, thanks for sending me all the chapters of your MEMORIES. I enjoyed starting from the beginning and reading again through all chapters. I

enjoyed them all but must say that the chapter on "My Father and Mother" I liked the most. When you brought up the name, Bowie family, I was disappointed that you did not mention the "Bowie Knife" that you told me about years ago. While this may be of a generation or two before you, I feel you still have bragging rights!! Carl

**From:** Marti Shea
**Sent:** Wednesday, October 11, 2006 10:45 a.m.
**To:** Lou Prentiss
**Subject:** Re: Father and Mother
Hi Dad,

Thank you for letting me see this first! Very nice story! And yes, just like their love, you cannot separate their story! You have so much to say about both of them; I think you have just touched the surface!

I like your approach. It's seeing the "insides" of the grandparents that I knew but not as you did. Of course I remember her "delicious" statements—she described her yellow lilies as such "aren't they just so delicious? I could just eat them!" And she is right! She took such delight in everyday things—such as watching the squirrels attempting to get to her bird feeder. I wish I had kept every letter that she sent to me!

And grandfather—I knew he was talented and played the ukulele (I think that is how it is spelled) and remember him whistling and singing at the beach. He had such a wonderful sense of humor. The funny grace he would say at the dinner table that would raise grandmother's eyebrows …!

Those moments you are recording are priceless and most welcome to me! Thanks Dad, keep writing!!!!

Love,
Marti

Chapter 16

## My Aunt Katie
### Jacque P. Markusic

The following are a few of many memories I have of my wonderful and loving Aunt Katie who passed away in 2010. I will miss her so much.

My memories of Aunt Katie span throughout my life. Because we lived apart in various parts of the United States and overseas, we didn't get to spend a lot of time together but when I was able to see Aunt Katie it was as if we had recently been together. I never felt uncomfortable around her because she always made it comfortable. She was always welcoming to me. My personal relationship with Aunt Katie grew when I was in college. I would go to DC during breaks and stay with my grandparents because my mom and dad were living in Germany. I would make my way to DC and Aunt Katie always came in to see me and take me to lunch. She would drop me off to shop in Georgetown and come back to pick me up after a few hours. This was a routine thing that would happen every time I came to visit during break. She was always interested in me, how I was doing, and how school was going for me. I felt a genuine love from her.

I always felt a connection to Aunt Katie and I think it was driven by our common interest in sports. I was athletic throughout high school and college and Aunt Katie taught PE. We had that commonality which later in life I was reminded of and realized this was what I just loved about her. This is what connected me to her. In 2005 I had the opportunity to go back east to Pennsylvania. As part of this trip I wanted to make sure I visited with Aunt Katie and Uncle Walt. My plan was to fly to Philly, drive to Frederick and come back to PA. Aunt Katie let me know she wanted so much to see me but wouldn't be home but rather they would be in Philly for the weekend. I told her that was perfect since that was where I would also be. Could we get together I asked. She and Uncle Walt were in Philadelphia for a croquet tournament and she would love for me to come. We were connected and so I flew into Philly, rented a car and drove somewhere just outside Philly. I arrived at the club just as they were sitting down to eat. We found each other from across the room. You have to understand that it had been many years since I had seen Aunt Katie but that didn't matter, she looked like I remembered her and actually looked so much like my grandmother, her mother. I spent the rest of the day watching them play croquet. I always thought croquet was a simple game you played in your backyard. I quickly learned there was a lot of competition to this game and it wasn't simple. Aunt Katie did exactly what I remember her doing. She began to teach me the game. She showed me the skills of the game and how to keep score. Before I knew it I was keeping score for her team. I remember her handing me the club and showing me how to stroke the club. This was no longer a simple childhood game; this was a competitive skillful game. Aunt Katie took this game seriously and I stood on the sideline watching her every move. I asked questions and she readily answered my curious questions. I ended up spending the remainder of the day and the following day with her, watching and learning. It was an absolutely wonderful time and a wonderful warm memory of her. We had time to visit and share what was going on in our life at that time. Again she was interested in me and how I was doing just like she did when I was in college.

When I saw Auntie Katie several years later at her daughter Helen's funeral she was so happy to see me, Barb, and Marti. She mentioned to me about our time in Philadelphia at the croquet tournament. She had wonderful memories of this time with me and specifically mentioned this to me. I could see the desire to experience this with me again and we talked about this. We never did get to do this but I know our time together was a special time and I am so glad that I was able to do this and that I had made the time to make it happen.

I have many other memories of Aunt Katie, including the times together with both our families at the beach and when they lived in Springfield, VA and we lived in Alexandria. We got to see and visit together, something we didn't get to do very often because of where our families were stationed due to military assignments.